Empty Arms

Coping with Miscarriage, Stillbirth, and Infant death

Surviving the First Hours and Beyond

Sherokee Ilse

Editor, Arlene Applebaum

To help you accept, yet not forget.

ACKNOWLEDGEMENTS

My sincere thanks and deep appreciation to:
My husband David, who shared his sorrow, strength, and love with me.

Arlene Appelbaum, my editor, friend, and supporter who gave me inspiration to continue. Bruce Moulton whose creativity and hard work ensure we always have beautiful books. Judith Benkendorf, Judi Levi, Marie Hagberg, Susan Erling Martinez, Gretchen Self, Ann Walker Smalley, Lynn Weigelt, Ronda Wintheiser who edited and made recommendations. Tim Nelson, always there with great ideas and support. Cathie Meyer who compassionately answers each call and sends the books out. The many bereaved parents, midwives, doctors, nurses, clergy, counselors, therapists, and friends who contributed in special ways.

To my loving family and friends who remained interested and enthusiastic throughout my preoccupation with this book and the work that I continue to do on behalf of bereaved families everywhere.
Most importantly, I thank God who inspired me, directed me to this work, and continues to guide me each and every day.

Graphics and design by Bob Wasulik, A Place to Remember
Copyright © 1982, 1990, 1996, 2002, 2006, 2008, 2015, 2016 by Sherokee Ilse
43rd Printing 2016

For additional copies write to:
Wintergreen Press/Babies Remembered
14108 North Biltmore Drive
Oro Valley, AZ 85755
(952) 476-1303
info@babiesremembered.org   www.wintergreenpress.com
email: sherokeeilse@yahoo.com

ISBN 0-9609456-6-0   (new ISBN 978-0-9609456-6-5)

DEDICATION

To

Brennan William Ilse

On November 2, 1981, one day past our baby's due date, we were told the most heartbreaking news parents can hear: "I'm sorry, your baby has died. There is no heartbeat."

Four long and grueling hours later we delivered a beautiful, peaceful boy. Our son, Brennan, never took a breath, nor greeted the world with a bellow. But he lived. And he will continue to live in our hearts and memories always.

For

Our two other babies...*Marama* and *Bryna*

who were miscarried, one in an ectopic pregnancy. Their premature deaths were early in pregnancy, but our hopes and dreams for them were real. We include them in our lives as special family members just as they should be. And for all the other sons and daughters, who were so loved and wanted, but who did not live long on this earth. May we all be joined in heaven or the hereafter.

Also in loving dedication to our two living sons,

Kellan and *Trevor.*

They continue to openly accept their siblings as a part of their family and boldly incorporate the ups and the downs of life, death, and loss in their own enviable way. They have grown into fine young men; we are so proud.

We are thankful for all of our children who each have given us beautiful gifts. We hope that by sharing our experiences, and what we have learned, we can make it more bearable and hopeful for parents and loved ones who experience this tragedy...those who are left with **empty arms**.

We wish you strength, love, peace, and the comfort of memories, which may sustain you over time.

Fondly,

Sherokee i David

Sherokee and David Ilse

If you have just been given the news that your baby has died before birth or will die shortly after, please read this.

What happens next? Slow it down.

The first thought most of us have is to 'get this over with as soon as possible.' Your medical caregiver, your partner, and you may feel this way. However, this is not usually the best path for most parents. What happens over the next hours, days, or even weeks, is critical for your long term healing and your family's. The entire experience becomes important in how you cope... making special memories is best done with some planning. We highly recommend you take time to create a *Birth Plan* which offers you and the hospital staff recommendations for how to do this well – the physical and emotional parts of it.

Since you are in **shock and disbelief**, if you go straight to the hospital right now to deliver, the decisions you face may overwhelm you, keeping you from really doing this well. Instead, if you are able to go home for a bit, hours, or even days, (if not, trust it will work out as well as it can) you can do some of the following:

- Home is a safe, secure place to cry together and to begin to prepare.
- Read materials such as this book to learn of your options and plan for what YOU wish to do to make this most special. Your hospital staff will also help you when you do check in. In most cases, they have been trained to guide and teach you.
- Get something from your doctor in writing or verbally that tells you what will happen in the labor process – medication and the consequences (will you be groggy and not able to remember seeing your baby?), natural labor, Caesarian, recovery, etc
- Call others who may be able to support and help you.
- Pack your bag, including such things as a camera, video recorder, baby clothing and toys for picture taking, etc.
- Get other children situated, and seek advice about how to involve them rather than keep them in the dark.
- Learn your rights at the time of the birth and afterwards (such as being with your baby as long as you wish in the hospital, bathing, dressing, and diapering, having your baby home to die or after death for a bit, naming your baby, etc.). Then begin to make a *Birth Plan* or be prepared to do this in the hospital.
- Find your courage and strength. You can do this, though it will be painful. Believe that you can and know that the upcoming decisions and time you have with your baby may very well be the most important things you do in your life.

Table of Contents

Emma

"There is, I am convinced, no picture that conveys, in all its dreadfulness, a vision of sorrow, despairing, remediless, supreme. If I could paint such a picture, the canvas would show only a woman looking down at her empty arms."

From the book, **Emma**, by Charlotte Bronte.

"Life can be the same after a trinket has been lost, but never after the loss of a *treasure*."

From the poem, A *Death has Occurred*, by Paul Irion

INTRODUCTION

Our hearts are broken. Our world feels like it has ended.

Our dreams, our hope, and our future

with this child are over.

Our precious baby has died.

Babies are not supposed to die. Not your baby and not ours. But sometimes they do die. It has happened, and you are not prepared for this. Likely, you are in shock and might wonder why it had to come to an end like this, because no matter how far along you were in your pregnancy or how long your baby lived, you love and want this baby very much.

Many questions and fears are apt to arise in all this confusion. Some of these questions are: What will we do now? Will this nightmare end? Who do we tell and how? How will we make all of the decisions that we are so unprepared to make? How do we plan a funeral that is meaningful to us? No doubt you feel overwhelmed... alone in your shock and grief and wonder if you can cope. Grief is a very lonely process. You must work through it on your own, but **you need not be alone**. Others can help you, even as they grieve themselves.

Because I have lived through the loss of my stillborn son, a miscarriage (a girl, I think) and an ectopic pregnancy (another girl, I think), I believe I can relate to some, but not all, of your feelings. I am deeply sorry your baby has died. I encourage you to make decisions that are right for you, just as David and I tried to do. Fight the pressure to do what others think would be best for you. They won't have to live with those decisions and memories. You will.

While there is no 'right' or 'only' way to do things, there are better ways. We hope this book will help you regain some control, assist you in making good decisions, help you create the best memories you can, and help minimize your regrets. No one can take away your pain; it is intertwined with the love you freely gave to your baby. No doubt you will come to feel that because your baby is so loved s/he is worth the pain of remembering, though no one wants to feel this much pain. You can build a special relationship with your child and your family right now that will be a solid base for long-term healing. And in a way, you can find ways, albeit different than you imagined, to become the

1

parent to this child for the rest of your life.

I wrote this book for mothers, fathers, whether married, single, young or not so young, as well as grandparents, family, friends and co-workers. Care providers are invited to enter into the experience of such losses, too. Some parts will apply to you and other parts will not. Find the information that will be helpful to you and share the rest with others who will benefit.

Most of the original version of this book was written during the first few months after Brennan's death, when everything was fresh and raw. Now, years later, I have expanded this edition to include a few other infant losses and pregnancy related losses not normally covered in such books. In addition, I have tried to include much of what I have learned over time and through lots of hard work. I have traveled this nation and world presenting hundreds of workshops to parents and their care providers—nurses, support group leaders, physicians, clergy, funeral directors, social workers and counselors. A special thanks to the thousands of families who have shared their stories and suggestions with me over the years. These stories add richness and more options to this latest edition.

David and I struggled, survived and grew from the painful experience of our son's death and our other two losses. So have many others. In the beginning we did not think this was possible since it was not easy or without many tears. But, amazingly enough, we did. Today we feel stronger as a couple, we have a new perspective on the fragility and preciousness of life, and we feel thankful for where we are now in our lives. I am confident that although you may not feel it now, you can do this, too.

How do I use this book and what is included in it?

If you received this at or around the time of your baby's death or impending death, *time is of the essence.* You will want to turn to the **Decisions You Might Face Right Away** section to learn about what is to come and what your options are. Often parents tell me that this is what helped them to realize the importance of spending time with their baby, even in death, to learn their rights and options, and to give them a chance to minimize regrets. Many of these decisions cannot be undone later.

If you are having trouble concentrating on reading or can't see through your blurry eyes, ask someone else to read to you. What you do now impacts you for the rest of your life, so I urge you to take the **Decisions** section seriously.

As you use this book for support over the days and months ahead, you will find there are many parts that will apply to you and some that will not. Skip those that don't, and go right to the ones that do.

Some people want to prepare for everything and read the whole book, cover to cover. Others start off by reading only the sections that pertain to their present needs, saving the rest of the book until another time. Don't allow the many sections to overwhelm you; take it a little at a time. Each person usually knows his or her limits, and I trust that you will use your own judgment.

Following the **Decisions** section, are some of the specifics of loss such as ectopic pregnancy, miscarriage, stillbirth, neonatal death, Sudden Infant Death Syndrome, or the death of an older infant or child. I include at least a little information on many types of reproductive and infant loss because thousands of people have told me that the feelings, needs, and coping skills presented in this book were appropriate to them regardless of the cause or timing of the child's death. These people are hurting and there are not enough supportive resources for them. What you feel is real, and you have the right to feel that. It is for you to decide how hard it really is. Don't let others tell you that your loss is less painful than someone else's loss. Though the circumstances of how the loss occurred might be very different, what is the same is the loss of a human life and human condition of suffering and sorrow. In your anguish, please remember you are not alone. You do belong. *Your grief is real and is valid*.

The middle portion of *Empty Arms* offers assistance with the concerns and issues you might face in the days, weeks, and months ahead. I have attempted to share many options by including pros and cons. You will notice, however, that there are some things I present as strong recommendations. These are things I feel deeply about which have been validated by thousands of parents over the past two decades. Parents continually tell me they wish they would have done these things or were thankful they made the choices that at first seemed especially painful to them. Even though I, or a professional caring for you, might promote a certain decision, take time before you decide. You will be the one who lives with it. Have an open mind, however. If possible, realize that there are long-term needs as well as the short-term ones. Most people try to avoid short-term pain. They don't realize that the

3

results of the tough, painful decisions may be the very thing that will help down the road.

Toward the end of the book I offer **What Family and Friends Can Do** and many pages of **Resources**. There are so many books, websites, support group, and organizations I could not list them all, but I did my best to get you started. Going to one website will be a door to many others. Reading one bibliography in the back of a book will give you more titles to research. Thankfully, there are now many resources to help you and your family.

Throughout most of the book, I have tried to add our personal comments in italics. We share our story with you to help you feel less isolated and alone and to hear our regrets and gratefulness. Maybe this will give you ideas and hope for the future as you take your own path.

David and I hope that you will share this book with your loved ones so they might understand their own reactions and feelings of loss and be of helpful. You deserve and need understanding and guidance at this tragic time. But remember that most people have little experience or formal teaching on how to really help someone during a crisis. They will not intentionally be hurtful, yet their attempts to comfort and advise you may not always be helpful, and you may want to give them ideas on what you do need and want to hear.

LEARNING ABOUT YOUR BABY'S DEATH

If your baby has died, it is natural for you to be unprepared, in shock, and to feel a wide range of emotions from disbelief to anger to intense sorrow. Whether your baby died recently or a while ago, you probably were devastated and confused. There is a profound sense of disappointment and loss when a baby dies. Your plans for watching your child grow and the life changes you were preparing for have been dashed. Your dreams, hopes, and future with this child no longer can come true.

This is an unfair tragedy! Whether you were pregnant for a short time, or a number of months, whether you delivered a stillborn baby or your new infant died shortly after birth, or whether your baby lived for a longer time, you have come to know him or her as a special person in your life. Take time to think about what your baby meant to you and how you are feeling now.

You soon will be, or already are, faced with many decisions. Give yourself permission to do what is best for you...even if that is different than what your partner, mother, or someone else wants to do. This is the time for you to say 'hello' to your baby and spend some time with him or her before you have to say 'goodbye.' People may push you to hurry and let go – to say goodbye and move on. Moving fast and avoiding the hard things at this time does not make the pain magically go away. That attitude usually results in poorly thought through decisions and regrets. Slow down, look carefully at the options, listen to what other parents have done, and then think hard about what makes sense to you. How you handle this loss will be different from how someone else handles a loss. You will experience grief, and what is critical is how you integrate your baby and this loss into your life.

When David and I were told that we would deliver our baby who was not alive, we didn't want to believe it and felt so confused. We kept hoping that it was a mistake. Only four days earlier we had heard a strong heartbeat. It all seemed so unreal so unfair. We had already experienced a miscarriage, which seemed unbelievable at the time; certainly something like that couldn't happen to us again.

5

EMPTY ARMS

We felt so out of control in a situation where we thought we had lots of control. Being that vulnerable and powerless was painful.

We had been so ready this time and were so sure that everything would go well. We had done everything right, and the love we felt for our child was very deep. Suddenly we feared they were right— our baby had died and we would have to face a life without him or her. I couldn't really deal with that until the baby was actually born. I had to get through labor, somehow, like any other mother. Once labor began, I tried to focus on the process and not the outcome. That was just too overwhelming.

When he was born, there was no cry and no nursing babe put to my breast. The silence cut like a knife into my heart, the anguish ran deep in my soul; yet the joy of birthing my first son poured out in spite of it all. I gave birth to our first son and it was amazing... full of intense drama and at the same time intense trauma and pain. Sadly, I hardly remember him now, and we didn't spend enough time with him. Not knowing our rights and what options to consider made this experience far worse than it needed to be and has haunted me for years.

Therefore, I am determined to reach out to you and urge you to keep your regrets to a minimum. Every decision matters, and this is the time you get with your baby. Fill it up; experience this mothering/fathering time to the fullest. Spend as much time with your baby as you can. Once your child is buried or cremated, all you will have are memories, pictures, and mementos to give you solace for the rest of your lives.

DECISIONS YOU MIGHT FACE RIGHT AWAY

Undoubtedly, you face many decisions. Depending upon the circumstances, your personal preferences, your resources, and support systems, there are a number of options and rights available to you during the upcoming hours and days. Many of the major decisions are presented briefly in the following pages.

As you contemplate these decisions, don't try to do this alone. Hospital rules should not require you to be alone; you may need to assert yourself if anyone tries to separate you from your partner and/or supporters during this time. Seek out your support people. This is what family and friends are for. Consider those who are good at aiding you in making your own good decisions. Tell them to come to see you and be involved. Don't try to protect them by doing everything yourself. You will build your support team from the very first moment. However, be aware...they may be grieving, feeling badly, and confused about how to act and what to do. Give them this book to read, especially this section and **What Family and Friends Can Do** toward the back so they will be on a similar wavelength as you. Do this immediately. People who share in your loss right away will likely become close to you, since you will be able to live the experience together and then share those memories over time.

How can I possibly make all of these decisions?

Trust and believe that you can make them. Make them slowly and one at a time. Everything does not have to be decided immediately. Make them in the order they come up, and don't think about the ones that are not yet relevant. For example, decisions about whether to go home right away or how to notify your entire circle of relatives and friends can wait awhile. Another decision that can be put off for a few days is the funeral and memorial service decision. While you may need to contact a funeral home before you leave the hospital or before the baby's body is released, planning the service can wait (unless your culture or religion has other requirements). Babies can be taken home and services/burials planned, even for miscarried babies. Depending

7

upon your state laws, you may or may not need to call a funeral director for miscarried babies. Some people wait days or weeks for the service to take place so mom is feeling better and can actively participate in the planning and the service. But don't feel rushed to make lasting and major decisions within the first few hours. Slow things down and take as much time as you can. This is the one thing you can do for your baby at this time.

Keep in mind that you and your partner may not agree on everything; you don't have to. When you disagree, try to find a way to meet each other's needs without giving in for the other person's sake. Some parents find one partner does not want to see the baby after death or take pictures, but the other does. Instead of agreeing not to see the baby or not to take pictures, possibly causing regrets and future anger toward one partner, consider this suggestion—the one who wants to see the baby should see and hold the baby, and the other who does not want to doesn't (though I strongly encourage you to since this is a regret of grieving parents.) Pictures can be taken and viewed later or not at all. But they ought to be taken (unless culture or religion dictates otherwise), since soon it will be too late, and you can't get them once the baby is buried or cremated. Though it may be hard to disagree, especially at a time when you want to be on the same wavelength, this decision-making will allow you each to be responsive to your unique needs and will be helpful in the long run.

The two of you will need private time together and a chance to talk things through. If you want more time alone, tell those around you. Do not worry about offending the hospital staff or friends and relatives. They want to do what is best for you and should understand your needs if you tell them.

Our family and friends were a tremendous help and comfort right from the beginning. We needed their support and are very thankful that we could ask for it and that they gave it willingly. We also spent much time alone with each other; we needed that, too. We feel we made some good decisions, but we do have many, many regrets, which haunted us over time. We needed more guidance and wish we had a book such as this to offer us the options giving the long-term perspective. Therefore, I wrote this book with that purpose in mind.

What follows are many options and opportunities you may now have. They are explored offering pros and cons and then we share our thoughts and experience. Due to your situation, you may or may not have all of the options available. Therefore, do the best you can.

We were told that our baby has died or will die. What do we do?

If you have learned your premature or ill baby might die, you may wonder how to respond and what you can do to parent your child during this fragile and scary time. It is your right to be with your baby as much as you can handle it, and you may even want to be the one to hold your baby during her/his last few minutes or hours. If your baby died suddenly, you can still spend time with him or her. This is some of your last time together; make the most of it even though it will be difficult.

If your baby has died even before the delivery, you may be told that for medical reasons it would be better to carry the baby until either mom goes into labor naturally or is closer to the due date. If this is the case for you, most likely it will be difficult and hard to understand why you have to do this. You will have to deal not only with your disbelief and grief, but you also will have to handle people's well-intentioned questions and comments about your baby and the due date. How do you answer a question about your yet to be born baby? Do you tell them the baby is dead or will die? Or do you pretend that everything is fine? Both of you might feel like hibernating until it is all over rather than deal with this. It might be difficult to see other pregnant women. All of this might seem unbearable, yet some mothers prefer this rather than having labor induced too soon. Many mothers have commented that at least their baby was with them longer, and they didn't have to face the harsh realities of death yet. In addition, many people use this 'waiting' time to plan ahead—to spend more time with the baby safe inside mom, to consider how to announce the baby's birth and death, burial options, as well as decisions about the baby clothing and picture-taking.

Waiting for delivery to occur naturally is not usually the only option. Many doctors prefer that labor be induced to deliver the baby rather than wait. They recognize that it is hard to carry around a baby who has died. The procedures used may be painful or take time to work. But some parents feel this is worth it. In any case, there are many factors to be considered. Seek second opinions about each option to arm yourself with information as you make good decisions that seem right for you.

David and I did not have much time to prepare ourselves for Brennan's death. We should have gone home for a bit to collect our thoughts and do some research. During the four hours between the time we received the news that he was dead and when I delivered, we did cry, share our sorrow, and talk about what we would name him, what to do about baptism, and who we needed for support. Some people wait weeks or longer and use this time to read such books as this one, to visit websites, and to talk with others about how they handled it.

Seeing and holding your baby

Seeing and holding your baby, who is dying or has died, is a most special time which can provide you with memories for the lonely days and years ahead. It can also give you a chance to share your love for your little one and help you say 'hello' before you rush to say 'good-bye.' Despite the sadness at the time, most parents tell us they are grateful for having seen and spent time with their baby, usually wishing they had more time. You will probably find it easier to mourn and cope with your baby's death if you have seen him or her.

Some people are afraid to see their baby because they imagine how terrible s/he will look. But you probably will find that as this baby's parent, you will have feelings of love, no matter what the appearance. This is true for babies of all gestation. If you are worried, ask the hospital staff to prepare you for how your baby will look. Have confidence; you will be amazed at what you can handle. In the long run, you may be thankful for having done this. Besides, imagination is usually worse than reality. One mother expressed her relief after seeing the remains of a miscarried baby after a D & E procedure, "Even though the baby is not whole, I can tell by seeing the limbs that this was really a baby. I had a baby! I am a mother!"

If you do hold your baby, take time to be alone with him or her. Unwrap your baby, so you will have a full memory of his/her characteristics. Check fingers and toes, open the eyes, try to remember the distinct features that make him or her unique and your own. Hold your baby for as long as you want; the experience of being close to your child is limited to a short time. If you desire to hold or see your baby again a few hours or days after the delivery; tell the hospital staff. You should be able to keep your baby with you in the hospital room for the entire time you are there which makes it easier to have private and extended family time with the baby.

Make the most of the time you have with your baby. There is so much you can do. Encourage family members and your other children to see the baby. Some families have brought in all the baby clothes and the camera. Over a few hours time, they dressed and undressed the baby, experiencing special moments that they had looked forward to for months. Other families have brought their baby home (or had the funeral director transport the baby) to lie in the cradle in order to have memories of their baby in his/her own room. After a few hours, or even all night (depending on your state's laws), they then had the funeral director take the body for preparation for either a home or funeral chapel service. It is amazing how many options there are if you let the doors be open, and follow your heart.

One family invited all of their relatives to visit them in their hospital room while they spent time with their baby who had died. Their coming and going, loving and letting go was much like an open wake. It took place over 3 days and 3 nights. After that there was little need for a funeral since it had already happened spontaneously in the hospital room. Remember, this is your baby. You should be the one to decide. A funeral director or the Health Department can help you learn about the laws that apply. Hospital staff should openly support such creative family involvement, remembering this is *your* baby.

Although some people will question these options, remember that before hospitals and funeral homes handled our dead, it was the responsibility of the family. Birth and death took place at home where loved ones were bathed and dressed. The review and funeral took place at home; the children and other relatives participated even to the point of digging the grave. Though this may seem unusual to some in the twenty-first century, maybe it is time we recapture some of our former sensible and special ways, which allow the family to make personal, yet difficult choices. The bottom line is: ***Do what you wish to do in your heart and don't worry what others will think.***

Maybe you chose not to see or hold your baby, did not get the chance to do so, or have forgotten due to drugs and shock. If now you have a strong desire to know what your baby looked like and pictures are not available, consider asking your medical caregiver or nurses to describe him or her. Maybe you feel okay that you did not see or hold your baby. Or you might regret it. Whatever you feel, try not to blame yourself or others for a decision that has been made and cannot be undone. You and your care providers did the best you could at the time. It does little good to replay it over and over, though it is understandable to have regrets about one or more of the decisions you made during this devastating time. Work to let go and forgive.

David and I treasured the opportunity to hold Brennan in our arms as we lovingly said hello and tried to say goodbye. I remember seeing him and holding him as a most joyous moment in my life, even amidst all the pain. I felt some calm and peace in those moments that are hard to describe. I always will be thankful that at least I had that. I know of too many parents who didn't get this chance or didn't think they could handle it at the time, only to sadly regret it later.

Now, years later, I do regret that we didn't spend hours and hours with him and ask for him again the next day. He could have even spent the night in a bassinet by our sides. Though that would have been painful in some ways, it might have been very helpful in others. Today I can't remember his face, his size, or if I ever uncovered him to look at his body. Memory fades, and the 10 minutes we spent were too few in the midst of the shock and trauma of the birth experience. If we had known it was an option, maybe we would have even taken Brennan home and invited people to see him there.

In both my miscarriage (Marama) and ectopic pregnancy (Bryna), I didn't get to see a full formed baby, though I'm glad I saw what I did.. Somehow, seeing made them more real. I did have Bryna cremated knowing she was too small to receive any ashes. What I have done is to look at pictures of babies that size and imagine my baby whole and at peace.

Taking pictures

Pictures provide you with concrete mementos of your baby. They confirm the reality of this little, yet precious life and give you cherished memories, which can help over time. Pictures also help make your baby real to family and friends who may not have met your baby and who were waiting with great expectations for this new addition to your family. The support you will need to live through this can be enhanced when people realize your baby lived and was real, rather than viewing this as merely the loss of a 'pregnancy.' Even if you think you do not want a picture now, someday you might wish you had one and then it will be too late.

The present standard of care at all hospitals is to take pictures. They should either have digital and/or traditional 35 mm cameras and film. Hopefully, they will take many pictures of you, your family, and your other children, if you have them...holding the baby, as well as close-ups. Ask about this; don't just assume they automatically take pictures since it is possible a few hospitals still don't. You may either take the pictures with you or ask the staff to keep them on file until later. A few people find it hard to view the pictures at first. If this is how you feel, they can be kept in an envelope and viewed when you are ready.

Especially once they are home, most parents comment that they seem to feel any picture is better than no picture. Interestingly, one of the most frequent regrets I hear is that people wish they had more pictures—at least a roll or two of pictures or many, many digital pictures. After all, the time with your baby in the hospital and possibly at the funeral (unless you take your baby home where you can take hundreds of pictures if you wish) will be the only times you have for taking pictures and they will need to last a lifetime. Why not have the nurse or a relative take pictures of the baby being weighed, measured, dressed, and undressed? Place your baby's hands in each of yours, put your wedding ring on your baby, have pictures of the feet, the ears, the nose, and of all family members surrounding the baby. Thankfully, studies of bereaved parents confirm that nearly all parents wish they had pictures or had more pictures. For decades, maybe centuries, babies had been honored, and remembered, in this way. Unfortunately, it had been viewed as taboo in our recent past and some people may still think this odd. Don't let such pressure get in the way of capturing precious memories with your child.

If your baby has some deformities, you, or others, might feel uneasy about having pictures taken. Something for you to remember when deciding is that s/he is your baby, and it is all right to want to preserve the memory with pictures. Besides, you may not even notice those deformities. Most parents notice the good things. One of the many parents I have met shared that she showed her pictures to friends and family for weeks when one friend asked, "What is that huge round mark on Jenny's stomach?" The mom responded that she had never even noticed that before. Obviously, she had seen her baby's picture many times, but was totally blocking that out. She looked at her daughter through love's eyes.

Recently, picture-taking of babies who have died or will die has risen to a higher level, even being featured on the Today Show and other programs. A United States organization, created by moms who wished for better pictures, called Now I Lay Me Down to Sleep (www.nowilaymedowntosleep.org) can often find a professional photographer in your area. (It is growing to other countries.) They donate their time and talents to help create beautiful pictures that are quickly becoming a standard, at least in some communities. Have someone contact them immediately upon hearing the news; it may take some time to find a person who can come to the hospital or your home while you still have your baby. In addition, there are artists who will paint a lasting picture of your baby from a picture (www.aplacetoremember).

David and I said, "No" when we were asked if we wanted pictures taken. We had a camera in the car and I wondered aloud if David should bring it in. He didn't seem comfortable with that, so I let it go. In my heart I knew I wanted them, but I couldn't agree to them when the nurses brought up the question. Now, I deeply regret the lack of photos, especially one of us holding Brennan. We have only our memories, which are fading over time. I also feel badly that my family and friends didn't see Brennan and can't even see him in a picture. Often his brothers have asked about him, and I wish I could make him seem real for them at least through pictures.

Naming your baby

If your baby died in utero, you probably have not yet named him or her. By giving your baby a name, you can officially acknowledge the birth and his or her place in your family. This helps your baby be more real to others and can help increase support from others who recognize that your baby was born and died. You will think about this child throughout the rest of your life; a name gives you an opportunity for sharing memories with others. You might wonder about doing this if you had a miscarriage, but it still can be appropriate because it says to you and to the world that this was your baby, an important member of your family.

When naming your baby, think about using the name, or nickname, you had chosen if you did have one ready, because that name really belongs to this baby. Another name for a future child will be special for that baby. One child can never replace another, and naming the baby might help to avoid that temptation. If you did not know the baby's sex, a name that can be either male or female, such as Pat, Devon, Chris, Erin, or Ashley can be used.

You might fear that if you give your baby a name you will feel too much pain and will become too attached. But if you loved, wanted, and carried your baby, you have already become attached. Be careful not to deny this. You cannot really minimize the pain and have a healthy recovery by denying the baby's importance. Giving him or her a name recognizes that importance. However, after much thought, some parents decide not to name their baby. This really is your choice. You may have a good reason not to do this. If you do not name your baby right away, you still can do so in a week, a month or anytime that is good for you. You do not need to rush into that decision if you are unsure. Just know that others may view a child with no name as a non-event over time, rarely bringing it up. At least that has been the experience reported by many families.

David and I are glad we named our son Brennan. When we use the name Brennan, it helps us, and others, talk about him, the pregnancy, the delivery, and our feelings. We realize his importance in our lives and that he was our first son. That was the name we had chosen before his birth.

A few years after our miscarriage, having had three boys, I decided that our first baby deserved a name and an identity. That must have been my girl and the only name I had been saving at that time was Marama. David did not feel the need to name this baby, but I did. I wanted to share my dreams for her with my two living sons. So we agreed to disagree and try to respect each other's needs. I named her Marama and he has had no problem with that, though he doesn't refer to her as Marama, or even as a girl.

During one of the many conversations with my young sons after our third loss...the ectopic pregnancy...they asked,"How many babies have we had and why don't we name this baby?" I remembered that I had a new favorite girl's name, Bryna. So although as a family we have not officially named her, in my mind, Bryna became her name to me. David did not feel comfortable in doing this, so we didn't talk about it a lot, but again, we worked to respect our differences.

Gathering mementos and special memories

Helen Keller's quote, "What we have once enjoyed and deeply loved we can never lose, for all that we love deeply becomes a part of us," sets the stage beautifully for the importance of creating memories.

When someone we love dies, such as a parent, sibling, or

grandparent, there is no doubt that they have become a part of us. We seek to keep them alive in our hearts and lives. The way we do this, which is a critical part of the grieving and healing process, is through remembering and nourishing their memories. We look at their pictures and share stories with others of things they did or said. We might have special mementos or things they made. Remembering them, crying over them, talking about them, and smiling because of them is very normal. That is what we do when we love.

The same is true after infant death. We loved our children and mourn the loss of all the dreams we had for them. The intensity of our feelings for them is surely deep. When they die so prematurely, society may urge us to forget, move on, don't dwell on the loss, or try for another baby. Sometimes we even do this to ourselves. This is an attempt to short cut the grieving and healing process. Yet, because our children have a special presence in our hearts, they are a treasure to be cherished, we need those memories. Often because the baby did not live long, we don't have many memories, so we need to dig deep for special reminders of them, and we may need to create additional memories and mementos.

If your baby was stillborn or died in the hospital, the hospital staff and most other care providers can help you collect mementos such as pictures, baby bracelets, a blanket, the premie cap, thermometer, a special poem, a sea shell, foot and hand prints, and much more. Many parents help bathe, dress, rock, place their baby in a bassinet, prepare for burial, and make a gown or casket for their baby...a few ways to create memories. With some imagination and creativity you, and those around you, can think of some wonderful memories to cherish and mementos to include in a keepsake book or box. Even if your baby died from SIDS, some of these ideas can add to the few memories you already have.

Collecting mementos has become a standard practice in most hospitals in the U.S and other developed countries. Most staff see the value in treating this loss like any other recognizing that memories promote healing.

David and I were one of many unfortunate families who received no mementos of any kind from our hospital. No crib card, lock of hair, baptismal certificate, certificate of birth, foot or hand print, or picture. We did not bath him, dress him, or spend much time with him. Yet, we did have sensitive people caring for us, which serves as a very warm memory. But that only goes so far when

I search for something tangible to hold on to, cry over, or smile about. There was a time when I felt sorry for myself and could only feel jealousy for those parents who had these things. Then I realized that it couldn't be changed, and I found myself searching for any memories or items that I did have and even made more over time.

"Where there are no memories, let the heart find the memories that would have been." Much like Sasha's quote after two children died a number of years ago, I found comfort by remembering my dreams for my children, imagining how they might look, reviewing pictures of when I was pregnant with each one, even if I wasn't showing yet. I was given a baby shower, and people sent gifts during the pregnancy and afterwards...all of these serve as memories. In addition, I thank Teri, a mother whose daughter Elisabeth was miscarried at about 16 weeks for sharing her most comforting memory. After lamenting over and over that she felt badly that she never held Elisabeth, her brother gave her a very special gift. He said to her, "But, Teri, you did hold Elisabeth. You held her within you for 16 weeks." I believe my babies (and yours) felt loved and held. That comforts me beyond words. And dads, you held your baby in your heart.

Baptism or a Blessing

What you ultimately decide about baptism depends on your religious beliefs and your personal needs. Many denominations do not baptize any children, others do not baptize a baby who has died. Some clergy have no problem with baptism, while others feel it goes against their theology.

Baptism might be a personal comfort for you even if you have always thought of it as only for the living. Or you might find a prayer or a blessing for your baby to be meaningful and comforting. Some parents have a naming ceremony or other appropriate religious ceremony. Consider talking with the hospital chaplain or your spiritual advisor before you make this decision as this may be different for each religion. If baptism is very important to you and no one will perform this little easy service, you can do it. The words used by most Christians are, "I baptize you in the name of the Father, the Son and the Holy Spirit." On the other hand, you could ask for a blessing asking God to bless and accept your baby.

David and I made the personal choice not to baptize Brennan, because we feel baptism is for the living, and we believe that God will bless and care for him even without baptism. I've learned recently that many clergy and chaplains offer naming and commendation ceremonies instead of baptism. I think we would have liked this, and it would have been nice to have a special certificate to put in his baby book.

How do I tell my other children? Should I protect them from the truth?

Although young children lack deep understanding about death, they are experiencing many of the same emotions you are. They need to hear the truth about their brother or sister. Share your thoughts and tears with them. They often have similar feelings of guilt, fearing that their wishes or thoughts killed their sibling. This should be discussed openly. Maybe they expressed feelings of not wanting a baby in their house or did not like sharing a room. Or if the baby was home for a while, they may have been jealous of the attention given to the new family addition. Even though you know those feelings of guilt are unrealistic, to a child they are very real. If they do not learn that they are not responsible for their brother or sister's death, they might carry those feelings with them as they grow up.

Many people suggest that children be involved in the loss experience. Invite them to the funeral, tell them what will happen, share your sadness, be open with them, and let them see their brother or sister if they are interested. You can help to make the experience special for them.. Explain to them that death is a part of life. Try to help them feel loved and included. Let them know that they will not die and you will not die now, which might be one of their fears.

Parents have shared their stories of how they included their surviving children, nieces, and nephews after their baby died. They often let the children help decide how involved they would be. Many held or rocked their dead brother or sister, or maybe they drew pictures for him or her to put inside the casket at the funeral. It seems that the children who have the opportunity to ask the questions that are on their minds and who are included in the experience are the ones who usually don't have nightmares or other trouble. Usually the ones who have difficulty are the children who are keeping things to themselves and not being included. They are left to cope and make some sense of this senseless experience on their own. There are many forms of expression and talking may not be something all children, or adults, are able and willing to do. Writing prose or poetry, drawing, and even puppet play could be encouraged. There are many books that can help children better understand about death; some of them are listed in the **Bibliography.**

Notifying family and friends

It will not be easy for you to call people and tell them your baby has died; babies aren't supposed to die. Feel free to call a few people and ask them to tell others; it is a way they can help and it can minimize some of the pain for you. Or you may find that repeating the story may actually be very healing and connects you to your support system.

Once everyone has been told you most likely will feel a bit of relief. Sending an announcement of your baby's birth and death is a way to notify out-of-town friends and relatives. This can be done in a simple and sensitive manner and can relieve you from the pressure of telling everyone individually. Putting an obituary in the paper is another way to spread this important news. Many parents have sent a card or notice to work and asked them to either post it or send it to everyone. (www.aplacetoremember.com offers beautiful announcement cards.)

An example of this type of announcement is: "We are deeply saddened to tell you that our son Brennan William Ilse was born and died on November 2, 1981. This baby meant so much to us. We hope you will understand and share in our sorrow and loss."

People will be quite stunned with this news and will have different reactions, anything from an outburst of emotion, to total silence, or a combination of these. They might say hasty words that you will not find appropriate or helpful. Or they might just ask you questions and be a good listener. Try not to take any hurtful reactions personally, and be aware that many people have a hard time dealing with death and do not know what to say or how to help.

David and I called many people during that first day, and even though it was extremely painful I found it did get a little easier to talk about after awhile. David called one of his brothers who then called some of the other family members. A neighbor called the rest of our neighborhood. Even though we didn't have to tell everyone ourselves, we were thoroughly drained after repeating the story a few times. I'm glad I made some of those calls, because it helped to prepare me for eventually re-entering the world to talk openly about Brennan. This also helped me to continue to adapt to the reality. I wish we had put an obituary in the paper and sent pretty cards out at a later date.

Mother staying on the maternity floor or moving to another area

If your baby died before, during, or after labor, as a patient in the hospital recovering from the birth, mom, you may have the right to choose where you will stay after delivery. Most hospitals will offer a choice, but if it is not brought up, talk with the staff about what you prefer.

You might find it hard to be on the maternity floor, because seeing the babies and hearing the crying is painful. Or you might need to be there because it validates your motherhood. Some mothers feel it will help them face up to it and not 'run away' from other babies; this could be hopeful amidst your grief. The experienced care from the obstetrics staff also can be helpful for you at this time. A number of hospitals offer a room away from the nursery and crying babies but still under the care of the maternity nurses. Once in awhile moms are placed in a room with other new mothers with living babies. If this happens to you and you have difficulty with it, be sure you talk with the staff about it. There often is another option.

I chose to move to another floor after I delivered Brennan, because I was afraid to hear babies crying and I didn't want to see the happy new mothers. I needed quiet time with David, away from that environment. But I never did get a sitz bath or the standard care for new mothers. In addition, the kind surgery staff had little experience caring for people like me. They were visibly distressed, and I don't remember any of them talking directly with me about my baby and our situation. I believe the maternity staff probably should have discussed the pros and cons with me. In retrospect, I wish I had stayed on the maternity floor.

I was not hospitalized when I had my miscarriage. I was treated in the emergency room and released within a half hour. This left little time to talk with anyone or even explore my options. With the ectopic pregnancy I was hospitalized for a few days and had outstanding care by the staff. It was at the same hospital and thankfully many staff had been trained by then to openly address the emotional and spiritual issues as well as the physical ones.

Dad staying with mom while in the hospital

It is generally wise not to rush home, since there is so much to do and the staff can really be helpful to you while mom recovers. You may want to be together at this time and have this right. If a private room is available, dad might consider staying overnight. If the staff does not offer, you can ask. This can be an especially close time for you; a time to grieve and comfort each other as well as discuss the decisions you need to make.

Perhaps you can't stay together because your baby was born alive, then transferred to another hospital and dad is encouraged to be with the baby. This probably is a very anxious time, with parents separated, worrying about the baby, and both probably feeling helpless. Or maybe you are able to go home to be with each other while your very sick baby is still in the hospital. Nevertheless, this is a difficult time and it is usually helpful to have your partner or a close loved one with you.

That first night was extraordinarily difficult for us. David and I did stay together and were able to share our pain. We felt it was so necessary that we were together in our shock and disbelief. We went back and forth discussing decisions, dreams, and going over what was happening. I didn't want to be alone with my thoughts, so I appreciated that David was able to be with me. We also used the time in the hospital to ask questions, review the birth with our care providers, and wonder together about a next time and our future.

Accepting support

It is common practice for hospital staff to offer newly bereaved parents support information. They will probably give you written materials that will be very, very helpful. Though it takes much energy, which you are probably in short supply of right now, looking over these materials soon is important. You may find literature for dads, children, grandparents, planning a funeral, and so much more. Often parents comment that they wish they would have known more at the time, but they put the packet away and months later learned about things that were awfully late in the process. In addition, the hospital may give information on support groups, other bereaved parents who can help (called Peer Support Parents), funeral help, local and national organizations, web support, and sites that offer jewelry, gifts, memory boxes and memory books, birth/death announcement cards, and so much more. Ask your partner, a relative, friend, or staff member to go through the packet of materials with you, or for you, while in the hospital. I believe you will be grateful you did not wait.

David and I gave birth to Brennan at a time when there were no resources offered. Thankfully, many of us have worked hard to change that. These days there are more and more support resources, yet the hard part is making sure that people get them and look them over as soon as possible. One of my wishes is that more experienced bereaved parents were invited in to visit and support the newly bereaved – either at the hospital or at their homes soon after the loss. (A recent study validates that almost 80% of parents wish for this support.) The few times I was able to visit a mom or couple in the hospital were incredible. Those parents were so appreciative; they felt less alone and knew that others had lived through such a tragedy and actually had some hope and happiness in their lives again. We were able to discuss the decisions they faced, making sure they heard the short and long- term implications of each one. In one instance, Sue and I became friends after such a visit...we'll always have that special bond.

Certificate of Birth

If your baby lived outside the womb, you should be asked to fill out paperwork that will ensure you receive a birth certificate (if you don't have one already) and a death certificate. However, if your baby was stillborn, the certificate issue is not so simple. More than half the states in the US and some countries do offer official certificates of birth, but many do not. You may need to ask about this since filling out the paperwork in the hospital is easier than working through a notary once you are home. To learn which states offer a certificate of birth resulting in stillbirth, visit www.missingangelsbill.org.

Why does hospital staff talk about my baby as a fetus or use other hurtful words?

You may find the word 'fetus' being used in the paperwork you need to do at the hospital or by some of the staff if your baby was stillborn or miscarried. Your miscarried baby may be described as 'products of conception' and some staff may even call it a 'spontaneous abortion.' This seems cruel to those of us who were preparing for a 'baby' and who have had 'baby' showers (not 'fetus' showers) and sent out announcements about our baby. If people use such words as these and they are offensive to you, speak up and tell them what you prefer. That is your right. On the other hand, some people can handle the use of this terminology.

Autopsy

It is wise to at least consider an autopsy, in hopes that you might learn the cause of your baby's death. This decision, of course, depends on your religious and personal beliefs. If your baby died outside the hospital (at home, or at a childcare provider's home, for instance) an autopsy will likely be required. Though there are still many deaths without answers, an autopsy may provide information, which can assist in determining how your prenatal care may be managed in future pregnancies or in the care you and your baby are given afterwards. Preliminary results may be done in a short period of time. A full autopsy report usually is not available for many weeks. You may need to call periodically to find out the status.

Most people are not prepared for what an autopsy is and what information is given in the report. It can seem very cold and may be difficult information to hear. Yet, with proper preparation you can handle this and any reservations you have may be outweighed by the importance of the information you receive. If you wish to know what is done to your baby during the autopsy, ask. It is your right to know.

Be aware that in some hospitals, there may be minimum weight requirements that must be met if a complete autopsy is to be done for stillborns or neonates. For example, because of technical difficulties in examining an extremely small, miscarried baby, the hospital may have a standard policy of doing complete autopsies only on babies whose birth weights exceed 450-500 grams (almost a pound.) Often, parents are not informed of this and wait long agonizing weeks, only to find out that a complete autopsy was not performed. Testing can sometimes be done from the placenta, cord, or other tissue. Thankfully, at this time researchers are finally taking an interest in causes of stillbirth, prematurity, and SIDS. Miscarriage is still a mystery and sadly, not yet a priority.

Having an autopsy may bring peace of mind or may leave many questions unanswered. If a comprehensive evaluation is done with genetic studies, tissue samples, and even x-rays, you may get more helpful information. In suspected SIDS cases, autopsies are standardized unlike other situations. Speaking with a genetic counselor may help you gain information that will have an impact on future children. Over half the time in stillbirths the actual cause is not determined, even with complete autopsies. One of the positive things an autopsy can sometimes do is rule some things out. This may be very important information for you. Have someone come with you when you do meet with the doctor to take notes and be another pair of ears.

David and I learned little from the autopsy. We never were called to have a conference, so when I was in the hospital one day for a procedure I asked to see the report. I sat in a little room, with a nurse checking in on me, trying to read this "foreign" report. Though I realize now that a physician should have made an appointment to go through it with us, at the time I was unclear about that and didn't question it. The report described our baby as healthy. However, it indicated that possibly the umbilical cord had attached to the outer edge of the placenta, maybe cutting off nourishment. This information was not that helpful for our next pregnancy, because we didn't know what to do differently. Since that time I have learned that the combination of poor cord attachment and my' nice, low' blood pressure may have put me at higher risk for an umbilical cord incident/accident. Dr. Jason Collins of Louisiana is diligently working with pregnant moms in similar situations (www.preginst.com.) And ISA (www.stillbirthalliance.org) is focused on stillbirth research and prevention.

Funeral or memorial services

Funeral and memorial services are for the living—for you, your family, and close friends—to acknowledge that this person was born into your family and deserves to be honored and remembered. It also is helpful for your family to be able to share your sorrow, sadness, and grief, along with saying hello and goodbye to your little loved one. Family and friends can be of support to you; consider having a ceremony or a service that includes them. This is one thing you *can* do for your child that will provide lasting memories, though it is not what you would have planned.

If you decide to hold a service, it is good for both parents to plan it and for both to be there. **Wait until mom is out of the hospital and/ or ready to join in. Or ask the funeral director to come there so both can be included.** A number of years ago mothers hardly ever attended the funeral. Generally, that seems to have changed, but still many mothers write to me and say the funeral was conducted without them. They complain that they were physically unable to leave the hospital, so they missed the planning meeting and sometimes even the funeral. Both the family and the staff need to know that rarely do **the actual services have to be done right away.** There is no law or rule that says this (though there may be religions that do). Ask a funeral director. Consider waiting until you both are ready to be involved so you can do it carefully and thoughtfully. You don't want this regret haunting you.

With regards to your child's remains, there are several options to consider. Cost does not need to be the determining factor; there are many things that can be done that cost little or nothing. Many parents admit that they hesitate planning a funeral or burial because they fear it will cost thousands of dollars. This is rarely the case. The costs involved will depend on the services used. Costs are usually related to the competitive climate in your community and ideally, your ability to pay. Many funeral directors around the country admit that if a family really has little or no financial resources they will let them pay what they can afford, even if that is nothing. Ask questions, call around, or have someone do this for you. It is worth it. After all, since this is all you can do for your baby, be sure you do it in the way that suits your true desires, one that considers your resources. Many counties or states have funeral benefits for people who fit certain low-income restrictions or are on welfare. Before you sign any papers or make a commitment, ask the hospital staff or county social workers about such options.

Basically the funeral industry is a service industry. You hire them to follow your wishes within the appropriate legal requirements. If you only want them to embalm the body and provide the casket, you can do the rest. Maybe you have a relative who wants to make the casket and another who offers to hold the service in their home or yard. You can do anything from having a funeral or memorial service right in the hospital chapel to a service in your home. One family had the baby in a bassinet in the living room and over 1,000 people came to see the family and say hello and goodbye throughout the afternoon. Your church is another option, as is the funeral home. I'd encourage you to have a visitation so others are able to see your child and have some point of reference in the days ahead about your baby...what s/he was wearing, who she looked like, etc.

Depending on your state laws and your personal preferences, you have many choices when planning a service. A funeral director can tell you over the phone what laws you must follow. In addition, they are usually sensitive and well-trained professionals who have experience in these matters. The resources and suggestions they offer should make this difficult task a bit easier. Some funeral homes even provide follow-up care and share their media and lending library with you and your family. There are organizations that may be able to help with finances for end of life expenses. One is www.angelnames.org.

Cremation and burial

Each state has its own laws about the length of time you have before the body must be cremated or buried. Few laws exist about miscarriage; you may even have the right to take their remains with you to be buried or cremated. Call your state Health Department or local funeral director who usually knows these laws well. If you have trouble, call a local support group or call one of the resources listed in the Appendix.

Hospital disposition, often described as cremation by hospital staff, is usually another option. Often people admit later that this wasn't really their first choice, but it seemed like the easiest. If your parent or 10-year-old died, would you let the hospital take care of the remains and never hold a service? Of course, making other arrangements is a most difficult thing for survivors to do, but it is one of the rituals of life and death. Be careful when choosing hospital disposition unless you are ready to learn what happens to the remains and feel you can live with that decision. Though some hospitals treat the remains respectfully, not all really cremate or bury the remains of miscarried or older babies. If you care to know before you make your decision, ask someone to be specific with you. Often, the staff has a feeling about what happens (or what they hope happens) but don't really know. It is your right to insist that they find someone who does. A hospital administrator may be called to help here.

The short booklet *Planning A Precious Goodbye*, (see **Bibliography**), is a wonderful starting point in considering the many options available as you do this one important thing for your child. You will even find poems, scripture verse, songs, and readings that could be included in the service. The book *Bittersweet: Hello, Goodbye,* is another resource packed full of service ideas, readings and resources.

Even miscarried remains, whether the body is intact or not, have many of the same options as a full term or 2-month-old baby. Now there are even 10-inch burial caskets for small babies. In the past, many parents have shared that they used decorated cigar boxes or music boxes, while other family members made the tiny blankets and gowns for their miscarried babies. These are still an option for people today.

Remember that whatever you decide regarding burial, cremation or the type of service to hold, it is your choice. It is not for your relatives or care providers to decide. Often parents are met with unneeded criticism or advice from well-meaning relatives when they try to plan for their baby's service. What may have been *right* for your parents 30 years ago, or what others would do if it were *their* baby, may not be *right* for you. You just can't truly know how you would want to handle the death of your child until you are faced with it. Don't let others talk you out of doing things you want to do.

We didn't do anything with our miscarried baby's remains. We didn't know we had an option. Unfortunately, I fully believe that the tissue and body parts were not cremated respectfully but rather treated like typical medical waste. Some hospitals do a good job and treat the remains with dignity and others view the miscarried remains as lab tissue with no special disposition. I wish I would have known then what I know now, but I didn't. I made the best decision at the time, or in this case, made no decision since I wasn't asked. I have learned to live with this information and the regrets. I choose not to be angry about it, but to try to change the system at the hospital and to promote careful decision-making with others who endure a similar tragedy.

With my ectopic pregnancy, we cremated the baby and we felt good about that. After Brennan died, we held an informal service and some family joined us as we said goodbye to our son. Though it was comforting to have these special people with us, we do have some regrets. We did not strongly encourage most people to come. In fact, we downplayed the importance of the service. We both wish we had done the opposite. This was the most significant death in both our lives. People should have come; we needed their support. We cremated Brennan and scattered his ashes at a waterfall near our home. The symbolism of the river flowing and life moving on was important to us. However, if we could do it over, we would have had a viewal so relatives and friends could have met our son. We also could have made him a special outfit, dressed him, cuddled him, and 'parented' him a little before we cremated him.

After our little service, we went to a relative's house for a dinner and a chance to talk. We were especially reminded at that time how fortunate we were to have such loving family and friends.

Now, years later I do wish I had a burial plot or place at a cemetery to visit. I could bring my children there on holidays, anniversaries, etc. I think I would decorate the grave and spend time talking with my children in heaven and my sons on earth.

Length of hospital stay

Mom, if you are a patient in the hospital, you will need to think about how long to stay. Talk with your medical care provider to decide when it is best for you to go home. But use your judgment, too. The amount of time you spend in the hospital will depend on your health, the type of delivery, and hospital policies. You might feel you will recover faster at home, or you might need or want the hospital care. If you stay in the hospital the normal length of time allowed after a birth, rather than leave right away, you may find some advantages. You can see your baby again, avoid hasty decision-making, and take time to learn of resources to help you. Going home soon means guests will arrive offering their help and you may need to begin dealing with daily routines. Maybe you are ready for this or maybe you are not.

With Brennan, I decided to leave as soon as I could, within 24 hours of the delivery, because I felt okay physically and I wanted to be home. However, now I wish someone would have encouraged me to stay in the hospital a little longer. I could have seen Brennan again and invited my family to visit us and see him. Maybe we would have felt we had more time to make careful decisions before rushing home.

Leaving the hospital

One of the hardest things you both will have to do is leave the hospital without your baby. Your empty arms will just ache. You also might be afraid to face that special, now empty, room at home.

Mom, if your baby died in the hospital or the last time your saw your baby was there, you might want to carry something when you go home. A keepsake such as the blanket the baby was wrapped in, the armband, or a teddy bear, might be comforting for you to carry. Or dad, you can bring flowers or a plant for mom to hold. On the other hand, you might need to have empty arms since you feel empty.

You may find returning home especially difficult if you have been hospitalized, on bedrest for an extended period prior to the loss, or if your baby died at home. Not only must you readjust to your home and normal environment, but to the sudden emptiness as well. It is like dealing with two major challenges at the same time. It may not be until this point that you realize how lonely and isolated you feel. There are no longer nurses coming by to see how you are, and you may find yourself suddenly very alone, even if you have other children or your partner around. Because of these feelings, it may be helpful if someone can stay home with you for a while. This may help you during times of deep emotion and help the time to pass more quickly. It also will give you someone with whom to share what you are going through.

David brought me yellow roses when I left the hospital. Even though that was far from what I had planned, it was somehow comforting and I did appreciate his thoughtfulness.

One thing I learned much later was that David and I could have probably taken Brennan home for a bit. I had no idea. We could have put him in his crib and carried him around the house, creating some memories for future. Our family might have come to see him. I think I might have wrapped him in blankets and dressed him in some of his clothes. Such regrets, if only I had known. While many hospitals may still be unfamiliar with this option, it appears that virtually every state allows this unless there is a communicable disease or it is a coroner's case – usually you just have to find the right people to make it happen. Even adults can be brought home for awhile (Decades ago all loved ones' bodies were kept at home. This still occurs in many countries around the world). If this is something you wish, talk with nurses, social workers, your clergy, a funeral director, or the hospital administrator. Sometimes hospital lawyers get carried away and make up rules for the hospitals that inadvertently infringe on yours. In other words, there may be rules that make this difficult. But the Public Health Dept. of your state or county should know – ask a friend or relative to help you call. If need be, contact me through my website (www.babiesremembered.org) and I will make calls on your behalf. In the unlikely event that you are unable to do this despite your desires and efforts, you may need to accept it and move forward.

DIFFERENT TYPES OF LOSSES

MISCARRIAGE

A miscarriage can be a very lonely, confusing and sad experience, not just for you, but for those who come in contact with you. It is a sudden, unexpected, and shocking loss that can shatter your plans and hopes for children, while your future might become clouded with doubt and anxiety.

A miscarriage usually is defined as the premature end of the pregnancy before the twentieth week and before the baby can live on his/her own. Most miscarriages occur early in pregnancy, usually between the seventh and the fourteenth week. Statistics estimate the number of miscarriages at approximately 15 to 25 percent of confirmed conceptions. Possibly 50% or more of all conceptions end in a very early miscarriage.

Many women are not admitted to the hospital after a miscarriage, depending upon the length of the pregnancy and the individual circumstances. Most often, they are seen in clinics, doctors' offices, day surgery centers, and emergency rooms. Medical care is given at the time and at the two-week checkup. Sometimes emotional support is offered then, too. After that it is usually up to the couple to handle their emotional needs.

Many people do not consider a miscarriage as the death of a baby, but rather as a fairly common occurrence and the end of a pregnancy, although studies show that about 75% of parents who have a miscarriage thought of it as a baby. The messages parents often receive are to downplay what happened, to get on with life, and to forget about it. These messages are usually intended to decrease the parents' pain and to promote hope. They are given out of concern and love, not to intentionally hurt. However, most people don't realize that instead of decreasing the pain, these statements often increase the isolation and loneliness. Parents get the impression they should not be upset and don't have the right to feel any pain. You know how you feel about this loss, especially if you see this as the loss of your baby and all your dreams. Yet, you are hearing such conflicting reactions from others, you might be asking yourself questions such as:

If it was 'only' a miscarriage, why do I feel so upset and disappointed?

Maybe you had an ectopic pregnancy, a molar pregnancy, a blighted ovum, a very early loss, or a later loss. Even though the baby might not have been 'visible,' or perhaps people had not yet been informed, you might experience feelings of disappointment, sadness, or anger. If you thought of this as a baby and not just a pregnancy, those intense feelings may come. In that case, you were expecting for and planning for a baby and now you are not. Your world has changed; it might seem impossible to pick up the pieces after such shattered dreams, or maybe you are not hit so severely. However, you may not be very upset if you didn't think of this as a baby, and that is okay. People will react differently after a miscarriage.

Typically, people will make an assumption that the length of the pregnancy relates to the amount of grief that you will feel. Therefore, the belief follows: a 9 month pregnancy loss is worse than a 3 month pregnancy loss which is worse than a 2 week pregnancy loss. Yet, you cannot measure the amount of attachment and love by the size of the body or the length you have known someone. Love cannot be so easily quantified and measured. Love is love, even if it was the love of the dream and the child s/he would have been had s/he lived. When someone you love dies, they are gone from this earth, and it is natural to miss them, grieve for them, and seek ways to keep them alive in your heart.

Besides, do men and women only become attached to their baby during or at the end of the pregnancy? Or does that process begin as children when they play the game of house; 'mommy, daddy, and baby?' Young children fantasize and practice being parents, as they grow they continue to picture themselves as parents someday. When they are young teens they often pick out names for their future children, especially girls. Even when searching for marriage partners, they may evaluate prospective partners as to what kind of parent they might be. Homes are purchased, neighborhoods and school districts selected, all with the future children in mind. Chances are that you have not wanted a baby only for a few weeks or months, but have been preparing all your life, even if this wasn't the best time. This may help explain why so many parents find themselves so sad over an early loss.

This was not 'just' a miscarriage; it was the death of your dreams, your hopes, your baby. Allow yourself to feel what is there in your heart and soul, to grieve, to say hello and to work towards saying goodbye. Let others know how you feel and what you need. Discuss the plans, dreams, and fantasies you had for your family and this baby. Find out how your partner feels and talk with other people who have experienced this. Find books that specifically deal with miscarriage as well as books and literature that deal with loss and grief in general. For further information you may want to read the book *Miscarriage: A Shattered Dream,* which I co-authored with Linda Hammer Burns. It is a short but comprehensive guidebook. Try your local library, bookstore or contact Wintergreen Press directly for this book and many other written materials on the subject.

We had a miscarriage at two-and-a-half months before we were pregnant with Brennan. David and I had just announced our exciting, though anxious, news when the miscarriage occurred. Suddenly we found ourselves 'unannouncing' the news to relatives and friends, which was very uncomfortable. They didn't know what to say to us, and we almost felt like we should comfort them.

People were sad and disappointed for us. Everyone, including the clinic staff, encouraged us with words such as "You can have another baby." But that didn't help me very much. If anything, it added to the hurt. However, David found those same words did ease some of his pain.

That was our first baby, our first pregnancy. We never felt the kicks or watched the physical changes as our baby grew, but nevertheless we felt an intense loss and an emptiness after the miscarriage.

We realized much later, actually after Brennan's death, that we had not really talked through that experience as well as we could have. We put our grief 'on hold' and tried for another baby. It did seem to bother David more and for a longer period of time than it did me. He had been very anxious to have a baby, but I had been unsure about the timing and whether I was ready to be a mother. So the intensity of our reactions to the miscarriage was different. Thankfully, after some time we did talk about those differences and came to respect that we grieved and reacted in unique ways. That helped to strengthen our relationship.

My third experience with pregnancy loss came abruptly one summer day in 1987. I went to the clinic because of a two-hour experience with intense cramping and nausea. Within an hour of the ultrasound, I found myself being prepared for surgery since an ectopic pregnancy was suspected. The shock of even being pregnant, let alone that the end of it was in sight, was overtaken by my fears

*of surgery, the potential loss of my tube, and concerns for who
would care for my children. A few hours later I learned that it had
been an ectopic pregnancy and they could not save the baby or the
tube. (Ectopic pregnancy means the baby is developing someplace
else besides the uterus, usually the Fallopian tube. The pregnancy
cannot proceed. If it is in the tube, the tube will eventually burst
and the mother's life can be endangered due to hemorrhaging or
infection).*

*Upon returning home, I felt numb and wasn't very emotionally
upset so I waited for the intense grief to come. It never really has,
though I did feel sadness. That surprises me, and yet, I accept that
those were my real feelings. I also had cried so many tears for my
other two babies that maybe there were few left. I do know many
other women and men who say that their ectopic pregnancy was
the worst thing that could have happened to them. That does show
how unique people are in their feelings about the same type of
experience.*

STILLBIRTH

If your baby was stillborn, it means that you had to say goodbye
even before you had the chance to say hello. The immediate and
intense pain of experiencing a stillbirth comes from the abrupt change
of feeling euphoric and high with anticipation to the unbelievable blow
of hopes dashed. All at once you have to face the news that the baby,
who was kicking and obviously so alive, now has died.

Until it happened to me, I had never even heard of stillbirth. It
might be helpful to understand the common definition before we go
on. In most states a stillbirth is the death of a baby anytime after twenty
weeks gestation, but this depends on the State Health Department
policies. Approximately one of every 100-200 babies is born dead in
the developed countries each year and more in developing nations.
Each year in the U.S. approximately 29,000 babies are stillborn. This
figure is almost four times as great as the number of babies who die
of SIDS, yet for years stillbirth has been ignored in many countries.
This is a relatively high number, especially when it happens to you.
Only lately has an interest in possible causes and prevention been
explored.

Are miscarriage and stillbirth really all that different? Is stillbirth
more painful because the baby was carried longer? Sherry Jimenez,

author of _The Other Side of Pregnancy_, asks, "What is a miscarriage, but an early stillbirth?" For statistical purposes miscarriage and stillbirth are separated by the medical community. Miscarriages are generally not recorded; stillbirths are recorded as fetal deaths but not considered a birth by many. They are not even recorded in infant mortality figures and have no legal status. Recently, however certificates of birth ending in stillbirth are being offered by almost half the US states and in some countries.

Sometimes well-meaning friends, family, and even care providers use the word 'miscarriage' as a way to define any pregnancy loss, including stillbirths. Using that term may make it seem like they are minimizing the loss of your child, perpetuating the myth that you won't hurt so bad if it is _only a miscarriage_. Who really decides when it is a baby and when it is not? Maybe the one deciding should be you.

Most often in a stillbirth the baby dies before the onset of labor, while the rest die during labor, or at the last days or moments before delivery. Sometimes death is attributed to a lack of oxygen; maybe the cord was not attached correctly, was compressed, or was around the baby's neck (according to recent studies, this can be especially dangerous if mom has what doctors describe as 'nice lo' blood pressure). Other times there might have been a problem with the placenta; maybe it separated from the uterus or did not provide enough nourishment. Or death could have been due to complications from physical or genetic abnormalities. Infections in the mother and/or baby are now being investigated; some physicians believe this may be a major cause of stillbirth. Other researchers feel some stillbirths are SIDS deaths in utero. Often the cause of death is a guess, even after an autopsy. Approximately 60% of all stillbirths at this time are unexplained.   Talk with your health care provider about what s/he thinks might have caused your baby's death; maybe they can at least rule out some things. Be sure to read the section on autopsy for further discussion on this issue. The internet will give you many avenues to pursue. Visit www.stillbirthalliance.org for the latest in research on stillbirth.

NEONATAL DEATH

If your baby died after being born alive, you probably feel intensely sad, angry, and bewildered. The anxious time waiting while your child struggled to live no doubt seemed like an eternity. You experienced the joy of pregnancy and giving birth, only to hear so abruptly that something was wrong. Or maybe you learned early in the pregnancy that the baby had severe problems and might not live. Chances are you may have held out hope that the tests were wrong, or maybe you spent time doing difficult things like planning the funeral or deciding who would be with the baby when s/he was dying.

Neonatal death is defined as the death of a baby anytime between birth and four weeks. The March of Dimes estimated the number of neonatal deaths in the U.S. in 2002 at approximately 19,000.

Neonatal death often occurs as a result of prematurity when the baby is born with underdeveloped organs or a variety of other complications. Abnormalities and birth defects might minimize the baby's chances for survival. An infant can look normal but have a congenital heart problem, a brain disorder, or other internal problems. Or a baby might have malformed features, genetic problems, or lacked oxygen for too long during the birth process.

Having a live baby who then is diagnosed with serious problems can be something you knew would happen or may come as a shock sometime after giving birth. Feelings of inadequacy, loss of control, and concern for the baby's needs and comfort are common and can be quite overwhelming. Thankfully, most NICUs (Neonatal Intensive Care Units) and nurseries have trained staff who can talk through these issues with you and your family.

When the baby is born with medical problems, emergency measures are taken that often include whisking the baby away to an NICU or maybe to another hospital. Many parents were separated from their baby, sometimes even before they have a chance to see and hold him or her. Mom may have been separated and missed time with Dad and the baby.

Parents whose babies have lived in the NICU and then died often wish they would have spent more time getting to know their baby and building memories for the long days ahead. Even if you weren't there as much as you would have liked, remember you survived in the best way you could at the time.

You may wish to talk with other parents whose babies lived for a while in the NICU then died. You may consider taking the baby home after death. Maybe your baby died shortly after birth and you didn't have the opportunity to see or hold her or him, especially without tubes. This might seem especially hard since you didn't get a chance to say your 'hellos' and its already time for the 'goodbyes.' Ask for pictures and for the staff to share their memories and stories of your son or daughter with you, in writing if possible. At least you can have a little something to remember in the future. If family members were involved ask them to share what they remember of your baby. In case you lose track of the staff members who saw and/or interacted with your child, your relatives can tell you whom s/he looked like and share any special features or moments.

Most people find comfort and positive memories in seeing, holding, and experiencing their baby for as long a time as possible. Of course, there are also people whose coping and survival skills at the moment will not allow them to go that far. That's okay, too.

SUDDEN INFANT DEATH SYNDROME (SIDS)

If you are the parent, relative, or day care provider who has experienced the death of a very special baby due to suspected SIDS, no doubt you feel in shock and emotionally drained. How could this have happened? The suddenness and total lack of control at having had no hint that anything was wrong is a unique bond people share after such a tragedy. The feelings of anguish, grief, and sadness are normal. You may fear that others wonder if you did something to cause your beloved baby's death. In fact, due to the laws and how police and pathologists approach this situation, it may seem as if others do think you did something wrong. When this is added to your own guilt feelings, which are totally normal, it can seem overwhelming.

Sudden, unexpected infant death occurs in infants between the ages of one week and one year and is diagnosed as SIDS only after all other alternatives have been eliminated. The deaths occur suddenly, with no warning. A mere few years ago, seven to ten thousand infants, or 2 of every 1,000 babies, died of SIDS annually in the United States alone. The numbers have decreased dramatically in the US and around the world in the past few years due to the international 'back to sleep' campaign. Since most families now sleep their infants on their backs, the number of SIDS's deaths have decreased by almost half. However, babies still die of SIDS. Even some who sleep on their backs still die and little is known about why. You may have done everything right, and now it has happened to your child. Or you may think that if you would have done something different your baby might still be alive. These questions are so very common, yet sadly cannot bring back a beloved baby.

An apparently healthy, bouncing baby put down for a nap or

bedtime and then found dead is a most unbelievable experience. This is followed by the trauma of calling 911, CPR, and the Emergency Room drama. Naturally, there is much questioning by professionals, often including the police. It is important to have people with you who can help you interact with these professionals. Do you have a close relative or friend to call during any of these meetings, even weeks and months later? More ears are better. You will have many questions and so will the professionals who are involved.

People hardly know what to say. Your family and friends will be angered and deeply saddened by the death of your baby, especially in this sudden and inexplicable way. The funeral and months that follow will be devastating. Memories of your baby's life will flood you and the 'what ifs' along with previous plans for the future may haunt you. Thankfully, your memories, although too few, will help sustain you and your family in the days ahead. You may find this hard to believe now. That's understandable. However, in time you will notice how important those memories are.

After the autopsy and questions have been asked, the wait may be long to learn the results. Usually the lack of specified cause, which then narrows the findings into the SIDS diagnosis, will be frustrating. Everyone wants answers about causes and prevention ideas for future pregnancies, though none of the answers will bring back your child. While research has been extensive on SIDS over the years, there is still so much to learn. If you think it would be helpful, ask your doctor to share the latest literature on SIDS. Call the national offices and any local resources you can find not only for medical information but for emotional support. There are many support groups, programs, and books on the subject. A good resource is www.firstcandle.org.

As you use _Empty Arms_ for support, you will clearly find sections that do not apply. For example, you will have already named your baby and may have had a baptism. But the section on seeing and holding your baby might be appropriate. If while at the hospital, you want to see your baby again before s/he is taken to the funeral home that is your right. My intention is for you to find what does apply and use that. Read those sections. You may also want to read the _SIDS Survival Guide_ by Joani Horchler for extensive information on SIDS.

OTHER INFANT DEATHS

Sadly, there are many other ways for a baby to die, from accidents and genetic defects to illness or other reasons. No matter the cause, you are a bereaved parent. While there are specific issues that you must deal with that are different from a baby who died of SIDS or shortly after birth from prematurity, the vast majority of issues you face other bereaved parents also face. Maybe your beloved baby had severe issues and you were asked to decide whether to end the pregnancy or not. If you did, you will have as much grief as anyone else whose baby died on a different timetable. No matter how your child died, you are overwhelmed with the suddenness of this death and wondering how you will go on. Grieving, no matter the cause, is intense and difficult. It needs to be dealt with and lived. I wish to invite you to explore and determine if this book is for you. We do have much in common and we can build from there. Read the sections that pertain to you, ignore the rest. I have included resources for a variety of losses, yet I know it is impossible to have complete resources due to space constraints.

ADOPTION

The sorrow and grief after giving a baby up for adoption involves many of the same feelings as other previously mentioned losses. Family members may experience such reactions, even though you each rationalize this as for the best. One of the different aspects with this loss is that it doesn't usually have the finality of death. Over the years it is common to wonder where your child is, even searching faces in crowds looking for him or her. There are more and more resources on this type of loss. *Tapestry Books* (in the **Resources** section) has many resources for families such as yours.

There is another kind of adoption loss – I have met many parents who were in the process of adopting a beloved baby and then something happened. Either the baby was no longer available for adoption, died, or something else occurred that made it impossible or impractical for this baby to come to your home. The experience of grieving for this baby will likely follow. After all, you are already bonded with this baby and created a place for him/her in your family.

If the baby died, you will have the added difficulty of not having many memories at all, few if any pictures, and the need to hear the details of what happened, since you did not live with the baby and can't make the situation real in your own mind. If the baby did not die, but is no longer able to be placed in your home, you know the child lives and may at times feel good about that, but you, too, will grieve for what could have been. On top of that, your loss may not be visible enough for others to see. They may truly believe that since you did not have the baby in your home you will not grieve as deeply. They are wrong. In any case, if your baby is missing from your life, you and others, will need to recognize that you made plans in your heart and life for this child. Now you need to work on saying goodbye. That will be hard and painful. Reaching out to others, finding support groups and books will be critical. You need and deserve support and understanding.

MOTHER

Mom, not only has your baby died, but you probably have had a chance to experience and feel your baby move and grow or you had time with your baby for awhile. The bond you had most likely was very strong. You might feel as if you lost part of yourself. You also might feel you 'failed,' in the sense of not bringing your living child into the world, something that apparently everyone else can do easily—or not keeping your precious baby alive in your home.

The emptiness you feel inside is something that only mothers can relate to. You ache for your baby, and sometimes your body acts as if your child is still alive. If the baby died before or shortly after birth, probably your breasts are prepared to nurse and the hormone secretion increases your emotional intensity. Your maternal love for your baby most likely began long before s/he was ever born or died. Your hopes, dreams and fantasies for this person were very real. In addition to the loss of your baby, you have lost a future with this special and unique son or daughter.

Sometimes you might feel very alone with your grief. People do not always know what to say or how to help. You and your partner are grieving. You will need to talk about this, probably for a long time. There hardly will be a day, especially in the beginning, when you do not think about your baby. Be gentle with yourself.

You may stay at home for awhile to recover. If you do go back to work soon, or on to other activities and interests, it will be awkward to talk with people. They will want to know how you are doing but might be afraid to even bring up the subject; that is natural. If it is important for you to talk to people about your child and this experience; if they do not bring it up, you might have to be the one to do it.

FATHER

Dad, most likely you want to take care of your partner, to offer support and love to help her heal and to ease some of her pain. At the same time you will have your own sadness and grief. Try to allow yourself to express feelings and to get support from others. You have a difficult role, and this will be a very emotionally trying time for you, too.

You will feel drained and confused. If your baby was stillborn, you were probably looking forward to getting to know your baby; the kicks and heartbeat had been exciting signs of good things to come. If your baby was miscarried or died early, chances are you could only experience the loss through your partner, so it is doubly hard. If your baby died in the NICU or at home from SIDS or another reason, you will also feel helpless. You might want to be 'strong,' yet you might feel like crying. Possibly your mate will want to talk about the baby, the delivery, the time your baby lived, and the death more than you will. As agonizing as it might be to discuss, you will probably feel better talking it through. Expressing some of your emotions outwardly might help your partner realize that you are hurting, too, so she will not feel so alone.

In the beginning it will not be easy for you, Dad, as you go back to work and face people so soon. They may want to know more about your baby's death and what happened but might be afraid to ask. You probably will have to bring up the subject many times in those first few days. You don't have to always pretend you are okay if you are not; allow yourself to tell some people how you really are doing. Be aware that you are grieving, too. You have every reason to be sad, angry, disoriented, or disinterested in your work at this time.

Though it doesn't seem fair, you will probably find many people asking you how your partner is feeling, making the assumption that you are fine or are not willing to talk about it. Many fathers have complained about this. One had a great answer, "Physically she is doing fine; emotionally we are both a wreck." This then opened the door for people to hear about his pain and to offer him some support, too.

BOTH PARENTS

Both of you should try not to feel frustrated if you seem to be on different grieving timetables and have different needs. This is not unusual.

In fact, it can work for your benefit. Some of the difficulty comes when one partner expects the other to feel or behave exactly the way *they* feel and act. For instance, if one is talking openly and crying quite a bit, when their partner tries to be upbeat, calm and quiet about it, the assumption is often made that the quiet one 'does not care as much as I do.' Each of you must be aware that how one expresses feelings does not always indicate how deep the feelings are. Both of you are tender and hurt.

Keep in mind that family and partners provide each other with balance on a daily basis. Seldom do they react in the same manner or feel the same. For example, one of you might be unusually happy, while the other one is really down. It will be no different now. Talk about those differences and find the similarities. If possible, respect the uniqueness that you each bring to the family; don't let this become another loss to you. If your partner or family members can't meet a need you have because it conflicts with their need, try to find someone else to help you.

When feelings are not shared, you might feel very lonely. Be sure to let your partner know what you want. Some days you will want to talk, or to have a shoulder to cry on; other days you will not want to talk about it. People sometimes have a tendency to measure grief by the quantity of tears or outward signs. Don't assume that just because one gets dressed and goes to work each day that s/he isn't still grieving. Also, if one of you cries often and is consumed with sorrow and pain, do not think that s/he will be like this forever. You are each different people. Let each respond to the loss naturally, without too much pressure to change and you will find your old self returning. After some time it will seem less stressful.

Tim Nelson, who wrote *A Guide for Fathers When a Baby Dies*, and I recently authored a new book for couples entitled, Couple Communication After a Baby Dies. This very personal guide touches on topics such as the roles of men and women, how personality and childhood affect partner communication, seeking the positive, the fix-it approach and its dangers, going back to work vs. staying home, regrets and guilt, and intimacy. Tim and I share our own stories with our partners offering our own successes and regrets in communication and togetherness over our 20+ years of marriage each.

As you work on your relationship, trust that it can grow and strengthen. The loss of your baby is very challenging and difficult, and you will need a strong partnership to recover and stay healthy.

Many couples experience a strain on their relationship. Give yourself permission to seek professional help if there is undue tension and if you feel you cannot handle it alone. A large number of parents do this and find it extremely helpful.

I remember sitting at home alone many days, feeling sad and sorry for myself. I tried to protect David by not discussing the topic that was so heavy on my mind. What began to happen was that the burden kept getting heavier, and I felt like it was all on me. When I finally would break down and tell David what I had been thinking, or how I had been missing Brennan, he admitted he had been feeling the same way. We would talk about it for a while, which always seemed to ease my burden.

SINGLE MOMS

As a single mother, you are likely to experience far less support from others and you probably also lack the support of a partner. Just as parenting a child without a partner is difficult, so is decision-making, grieving, and healing after the loss of a baby. No matter what the circumstances of this pregnancy, if the father is not around to support you it may feel like an extra burden on your shoulders. It is likely that people will state or insinuate that you are lucky it happened this way because single parenting might have been too much for you. Or in trying to rationalize this, they may suggest that caring for a less than perfect baby would have been awfully hard; therefore it is better this way. Issues such as financial problems may be brought up.

What they may be avoiding, or ignoring, is the emotional attachment that grows between mother and child and the painful response that follows the separation. Right now, you need to find people who will understand you, support you, and allow you to feel and grieve. You are a parent who happens not to have a partner, but you need what other bereaved parents need, plus more.

If you are a teen, you may get even less support. Friends may expect you to go back to your *normal self* and may want you to party with them, do homework with them, talk of dating and other daily routines that may seem trivial to you. People will suggest that this is your chance to go back to innocent childhood, school, and time to build a better future for yourself.

Even though you may wish this to be possible, in reality you have experienced a crisis involving motherhood, which is one path to adulthood. It is probably impossible to go back to the innocent person you were before. In some cases, it now means you lose your chance at your own apartment, autonomy, and respect from others as a capable adult. Now, you may have to continue living at home with curfews and rules. Not only have you lost your parenthood and your baby, but your independence and your *near*-adult status.

Some teens get married or stay married after their baby's death. People might question that and encourage you to go back to the single life, since you no longer have parenthood in your near future. This decision needs to be carefully discussed between the two of you and your families if that is appropriate. Just because there is no living baby does not mean you have to split up, nor do you need to stay together for the sake of anyone but yourselves.

Whether you are a teen or an older mom, you will still no doubt feel the emptiness and sadness that comes with having a child die. Your age does not necessarily make it easier for you to accept this. Link up with support groups and other single moms who have had similar losses. Seek assistance from your church or your community resources. Try to find reading material. Take it slowly, care for yourself, and try not to let the poor advice of others stop you from doing what is best for you. Keep believing in yourself, and have hope for the future, though that may seem difficult some days.

There are two books on the market that you might find helpful if you are a single mom. They are *__Single Parent Grief__* which I wrote and *__After the Loss of Your Baby: For Teen Mothers__*, by Connie Nygiel.

THE FIRST DAYS AND WEEKS

Initial reactions

The minutes, hours, and days have a tendency to jumble together, and you probably feel disoriented, confused, and vulnerable. By now your shock might be starting to wear off and the pain, loneliness, and other intense emotions will follow. You might feel extremely sad one moment and full of anger at the 'unfairness of it all' the next. This is common.

You may find yourself sighing or moaning often. Many people describe a heaviness and tightness in the chest that feels like a real heartache. These are normal grief reactions from emotional trauma.

In addition to your emotional responses, Mom, you may experience the normal physiological responses to the end of the pregnancy, with the hormonal changes. For example, if your baby was stillborn or died shortly after birth, and in many cases even after miscarriage, your body will still respond as it would after a normal birth. Hormonal changes following pregnancy can cause mood swings and even postnatal depression. Your breasts may become painfully enlarged with milk, milk that is regrettably not needed. Your breasts may actually leak. This provides another harsh reminder of the loss of your baby. Within a short time, as long as you avoid stimulation, the breasts will gradually diminish in size and the milk production will cease. There are natural ways of wrapping your breasts that can stop or limit the milk. Your medical care provider may mention medication to stop the milk production. There may be some side affects to it, however, so do ask about that. Some mothers have found it therapeutic to offer their milk to a milk bank rather than wait for it to dry up.

Many times during those first few days and weeks I remember wondering what was happening to me. I sat around and sighed continuously, experiencing a tightness in my chest and a heaviness in my heart, making it difficult to breathe at times. I didn't have any control of my emotions and had a hard time concentrating on anything—anything, that is, except my baby and our family, which was robbed of an important member. Nothing else seemed to matter; not work, not other people. I couldn't make myself care about anything else. I felt as if I was not in control of my mind or my body; everything seemed to be just happening to me. I forgot many things, probably due to the fact that I just really couldn't care about anything else. I was not in control of my mind or my body; everything seemed to be just happening to me.

David and I were very confused and had a hard time making decisions. We had a tendency to just say no to everything rather than try to make a rational decision or think the situation through. I remember that my parents called to ask if they could visit us during those first few days. We said, "No, you don't have to do that. We can manage." We couldn't even think about what their suggestion meant; it was just easier to say no. After we talked it through, we wished we had said yes, because we knew it probably would have helped if they were there. Luckily, they did not really believe we had meant no and called back to ask us again. That time we agreed, and we were so glad they did come to be with us for a few days.

It is very easy to feel absolutely alone and helpless at this time, even if there are many people around. I have included some questions and comments to help prepare you for some of the feelings you might have and things you can do to get through these difficult days.

I feel so sad and lonely and cheated and angry. Am I going crazy?

Are you going crazy? No, but the feelings and behaviors can look like that. Instead you are grieving, a normal process that happens when you love someone deeply and s/he dies. Grief symptoms and feelings are much like going 'crazy' or like you are 'losing it.' This is often troubling to people who do not understand grief. It is overwhelming to have the unthinkable happen. Emotions and shock take over, and often cannot be controlled. One mother stated that she wanted to put a bumper sticker on her car that said, "I'm not crazy, I'm grieving!!"

At any time you might feel very depressed, angry, sad, withdrawn, or just drained and empty. Forgetfulness, having trouble speaking complete sentences, losing things, feeling physically sick, sobbing uncontrollably, or feeling numb and distant is a sampling of what you can expect. To add to the list are feelings of disbelief, bargaining, anger, sadness, guilt, and loneliness (I probably forgot a few). And yet, you may also move in and out of humorous moments, loving memories, and thoughts of gratefulness for such things as having had the time you did with this baby or having a loving family. You may bounce around and experience many of these emotions in one day or at any time. After all, the drama and trauma of new life, love, and then death are intense and confusing.

Many people believe that if they just survive enough to let time pass they will get better. The idea that each day gets a little better, like climbing a ladder, is a myth. Grieving and healing is not an upward, controllable process (unfortunately.) Unlike climbing the ladder, which soon gets you to the top, grief is much more like a wild roller coaster ride or a stormy sea. It has its ups and downs, and at times you feel like you are drowning. There seems to be no exact pattern. Just when you think you are entering a lengthy calm another wave hits from behind. Eventually some peace and beauty will be more visible, but maybe not right away or for too long.

The grieving and healing process is a long process, a dark tunnel of sorts, after all you love your baby deeply, it will hurt for a long time. Most people agree that it can't be done quickly and that it seems to last a long time. There is usually little you can control, but go ahead and try if you wish. Having supportive people around and doing good things for yourself can help. In a way, people, memories, and treating yourself well, can be like lit candles in the your dark tunnel, lighting the way and giving you comfort.

In his book *Don't Take My Grief Away*, Doug Manning has a wonderful passage about grief, "Grief is not an enemy, it is a friend. It is a natural process of walking through the hurt and growing because of the walk. Stand-up tall to yourself and to your friends and say, 'Don't take my grief away from me, I deserve it and I'm going to have it.'"

Don't try to avoid the hard work of grief, though that is a very common coping technique. Instead, prepare yourself for hard times and let the waves carry you, while you keep your head above the water. Go with the flow; don't expend too much energy fighting it since you will need so much energy just to tread water. The ability to swim again will come.

Some days will be much harder for you than others, but as time goes by those bad days will not overwhelm you as often. Don't be surprised if it takes a long time, months and months, for you to feel significantly better. Though expect some feelings of loss for years and years. If I can do it and thousands like us can do it, you can, too.

Have some hope. Even years after a loss, bereaved people comment that they feel much better, but they haven't totally forgotten. There are occasional times when they recall the tunnel experience. Yet, they don't dwell on it every day or very often.

It is important that you express your feelings and allow yourself to grieve in whatever way you need. You probably will feel healthier if you express your emotions and do not keep them inside. Everyone copes differently. You might be tired and lethargic, might need to get busy right away, or might need to scream the pain and anguish out loud. Do not box yourself in, as if you have to fit a pattern. And if you do a few 'crazy' things, well, accept that and laugh about it later.

For now though, you can expect to feel very confused emotionally. All of these feelings of craziness do not mean you are crazy. However, if you do feel overwhelmed, seek assistance from someone, either a family member, your clergy, a grief counselor, the hospital chaplain, or the social service department.

Why me? Why us? It isn't fair!

There is no rational reason why you or why us. Your loss is terrible, and you are right, it is not fair! This might be the first time a baby of yours has died, or it might not be. Each time is devastating, and each time the unfairness of it all strikes again.

You might wonder how this can be happening to you. Some people believe that they did something to deserve this; maybe a past sin, an abortion earlier in life, feelings of not really wanting this baby, or even unusual things like drinking too much soda. It is not because you deserve it or because you are an unfit parent or even that you made mistakes and were not perfect. It just happened. As difficult as that is for you to accept, it seems true.

Why would God do this to me? A loving God would not have allowed this to happen!

No human being can really answer this outcry of injustice and confusion over God's role in such a tragedy. Some people do believe they are being punished and cannot be convinced otherwise. Others believe that in this imperfect world where God allows pain and suffering, He is there to comfort and offer support. Still others do much soul-searching and reach out to their clergy, the Bible, and to God, trying to understand and seek peace. Many find new meaning to life while some find themselves moving away from God and their previous faith. This is a very personal and painful path for most people who have faith and believe in God. Try not to give up too easily. It may take much time, work, searching, and pure faith to continue a strong relationship with God and your church while working on acceptance of the terrible loss of your child.

You might have a hard time coming to terms with this tragedy in relationship to your religious faith. You might feel angry with God, as many people do, when confronted with tragedy. Some people will tell you that if you had strong faith you would not be angry with or blame God. It is not wrong or bad for you to be angry with God. He can handle it and probably accepts it for what it is, understanding this expression of a very human emotion. It is all right to express any anger, blame, or the betrayal you are experiencing, rather than keep them inside. Let them out and work towards eventual peace. Take the time to talk this out, with your clergy, family, or friends. Support can come for you now from your religious community and your faith.

You soon will be aware of the conflicting beliefs people have concerning God's role in your baby's death. Other people's comments might help or confuse you. Typical ones are, "God must have thought she was pretty special to have wanted her with Him," or "God did not 'take' him, He was there to 'receive' him," or "God is hurting as much as you are. He is not responsible for her death," and "He needed some young angels, too." Once you have a sense of your own personal philosophy, in time you will recognize that some comments help, some do not. People are trying, as unsuccessful as their "help" might be, because they care about you.

No matter what your religious background or beliefs you might consider using prayer as a healing power. Ask others to pray for you, your child, and your family. Some people find immense comfort in visualization and imaginative prayer or meditation. For example, mom or dad imagines their baby in heaven, happy, and at peace in the arms of Jesus, or with other loved ones who have died. One mother stated, "In this kind of prayer there is an opportunity to tell the child all the things we never had a chance to say. This is a very deep experience that only begins as a pretend game and it seems that God 'takes over' and provides what we need to comfort and heal us." This kind of praying is described in a book by Francis and Judith MacNutt, *Praying for Your Unborn Child*. The book teaches parents how to pray during the different phases of pregnancy and includes a chapter at the end on miscarriage and abortion.

Many people have commented that they found comfort in the realization that God knows what it is like to have a child die. After all, His son Jesus suffered and died. How could He ever purposely inflict that same anguish on others? Of anyone, He is the one to look to for true comfort, understanding, and strength.

Whatever your belief about religion and God, seek out clergy (even if it is not your own), your faith family, and others to give you the support you might need now. They will not have the answers, maybe no one on earth does, but they may shed some light, share an insight, or just listen, all of which may help you deal with this a little better. Many clergy are sensitive to these issues and may be able to offer you caring support. Some people feel the book _When Bad Things Happen To Good People_ by H. Kushner is a helpful book, especially if they believe that God did not choose them and make this happen. Instead it happened and He was there for support in time of trouble. Not all people believe this nor does everyone find comfort in this book. Find what makes sense to you or what you feel is true.

How will we react toward each other? My partner does not seem to understand how I'm feeling.

Everyone grieves differently, because everyone has individual needs. Each parent experiences the loss in a unique and personal way. It might be helpful to consider each person's feelings and needs. Keeping communication open is a key right now and in the days ahead. Be open and honest, and respect how you are similar and different from each other. In our book, _Couple Communication After a Baby Dies: Differing Perspectives_, Tim Nelson and I have devoted an entire 100 pages to this important subject. While I can't give a thorough discussion of re-lationships here, you may want to consider some of the following topics.

Am I a parent or not?

If this was your first child, you might be unsure. You are not the 'practicing' parents you had expected to be. You have spent months, maybe years preparing to parent this baby. Now here you are, a mom or dad, with no baby. Or if you had a baby with you at home for a while and now since her/his death you are home alone, you may wonder if you can still be described as a parent. The answer is clear—of course you are a parent, one who has suffered the ultimate tragedy, the death of your beloved child.

You will want people to acknowledge that your baby lived and died, so you could have urges to shout from the rooftops or wear a sign saying "I am a parent," or "My baby died." You are different because of this, and you never again will be quite the same.

By talking openly about your baby, in some ways you help yourself and others accept your parenthood as you work through this. Others will pick up on the cue that you want to talk about it and not ignore it. You will find other mothers who will talk about delivery, sickness during pregnancy, the 'first' days, and other details. Fathers can talk to one another about their role, fears, support, and the like. If you had your baby home, you can talk about the first smiles, yawns, and other special times.

In my opinion, after Marama and Brennan's death I was a mother; I just didn't have a baby at that time. The memory of my children lived with me, then, today, and always. On that first Mother's Day after Brennan died, I expected cards to acknowledge my motherhood. I had been initiated into motherhood in the most painful way, certainly I deserved a corsage, a card, or some special validation. I should have told a few people of my need. Maybe they would have followed through. I was touched that David remembered me with a card and special thoughts. A few friends did check in with me, which also meant a lot to me. It was a very sorrowful and hard day for me. I made sure that I supported David in a similar fashion on Father's Day.

As I add to the revised edition, I can share the perspective of now having living children. My two living sons are a blessing and people now treat me like a mother. The very first Mother's Day after Kellan's birth I received a few cards that started off, "Congratulations on your first Mother's Day." It hurt me to think that people believed that only then did I "graduate" to motherhood. Yet, I tried to understand that they were thrilled that we finally had a living child and were trying to express this in a card. Still years later, on special anniversaries and days such as Mother's and Father's Day some of the painful feelings join with the joyous ones as we celebrate.

I feel so guilty. Is this normal?

Guilt probably is one of the most common and intense feelings parents have after the death of their child. It is a normal part of grief. People have guilt feelings almost every day of their lives. This seems to be a human condition. Yet, when that guilt results from a very serious situation such as this, it can seem so abnormal. Maybe it is not so bad to expect some guilt or regret and try to deal with it knowing that everyone does the same thing. Just don't let it get out of hand.

As a parent, it is common to wonder if there was something you could have done to prevent this from happening, or if you did something that might have caused this. Mom, you might spend hours going over your actions in the days before the baby died. If the baby died in utero, both of you might wonder if sexual activity was the cause. Or if you had feelings of uncertainty about whether you really wanted a child or whether the time was right. You might feel strongly responsible for your baby's death if you feel you did not check on him/her often enough or just having your baby in daycare. Chances are that both of you might feel some guilt and you should discuss that, trying not to blame yourself or each other.

Don't be too hard on yourselves by going over and over what you could have done differently. If the 'what ifs' eat away at you for too long they can damage your self-confidence and your relationships. Try to keep guilt under some control and expend your energy on coping, grieving, and working through this tragedy. You did the best you could, and so much was out of control. Maybe now what you can try to control is how much the guilt and regretful feelings will affect you.

I must say, I often wondered if I did something during those last few days to cause Brennan's death. As his mother, I was supposed to keep him safe, yet my body failed me. I also remember feeling guilty and wondering if maybe my jogging and exercise classes had been the cause of Marama's miscarriage. I know these are normal feelings, but after awhile they can become destructive. I worked hard on letting go and forgiving myself even for the smallest things (like running too much, dancing the weekend before Brennan's death, previous sins, etc). It helped to talk out these feelings with my medical care provider and with David. I came to believe that I really didn't do anything to cause either death, they just happened, and my feelings of guilt and self-blame didn't help at all.

Secretly, I blame my partner because our baby died.

Blame is similar to guilt, but can be directed at someone else. It is not uncommon to search for someone to blame. Blaming is a reaction to your own feelings of helplessness. Your baby's death is not your partner's fault. Thoughts and actions could rarely be the cause of the death.

Your anger needs to be expressed in some way, and you may lash out at your partner or someone close to you. This anger, in the form of blame, can be a very destructive force in your relationship. Do find appropriate ways to express your anger while trying to work together. Try to have compassion for each other during this stressful time, and work towards forgiving and letting go. Talk these feelings through or seek help from a professional.

I feel so glad that David didn't blame me, nor did I blame him, since we already had so much to deal with. It was a relief for me to know that he didn't feel it was my fault. Many parents have commented that they did feel blamed either by their partner or relatives. Sometimes quick comments made in conversation promoted these feeling— comments such as, "You won't exercise so much during your next pregnancy, will you?" or "Next time you'll go to see the doctor sooner if you suspect problems, won't you?" Though it may not be the intention to blame you, when you are extra sensitive and vulnerable, it can seem that this is what is happening.

Can I forgive myself and others?

In order to stay healthy in the short term and especially over time, it is imperative that you find peace and reduce your stress. There is much evidence that holding onto pain, regret, anger, and blame of self and others can poison your body and lead to serious illness.When you are able to forgive, allowing love to be dominant, you give good health a chance.

One mom wrote that she realized over time, long after her divorce, that she finally had forgiven her husband for many things pertaining to their son's death and their grief journey. She wrote, "I forgive him for the many things that I can now understand were his way of coping. His need for dominance and unquestioned obedience were probably the only way he thought he could ward off the pain and maintain control. The longer he refused to acknowledge his grief, the harder he had to try to maintain the control." This couple split up partly because of the differences in how they handled problems such as this. You may also have different coping styles and may need to work on 'letting go' of your frustrations and regrets in how you each handle this.

The hardest person to forgive is usually yourself. You may perceive you have done something wrong or that you didn't notice a significant piece of information. Maybe you believe that if you had gone in sooner or had extra testing that your baby might have lived. Some parents regret saying things in the heat of intense emotions to their partner or others that was hurtful. In retrospect, you did the best you could at the time with what you knew. The past cannot be changed. If you continue to let it haunt you, it will hurt you and others even more in the future. Pray for the gift of forgiveness of your blame. Give it up. Give it to God. Give it away. Even if you never send it, write a letter to the person you hurt, or to your child, or to yourself, and ask to be forgiven. Believe you can move beyond this and focus on the things that you can do and say now to heal and to move forward positively. If you want to, and if you understand the importance of this, you can and will when you are ready. Forgiveness is a gift, not so much to others, but rather to yourself. By releasing the blame, you free your heart from tension and stress. If you really find you are stuck and cannot move on, seek counseling.

I'm sure I still feel my baby kick or cry at night. How can this be?

You are not going crazy. This is a very real phenomenon. Many mothers whose babies died in utero or very shortly after birth are quite certain that they feel the baby kick, even days and weeks later. As a mother whose baby has died, you might unconsciously want to believe the kicks are real, because you have a need to feel life. Whether these are gas pains, stomach gurglings, or imagined feelings, many mothers have shared that they seem real. Often mothers wake up, insisting they hear the baby cry. Probably you are dreaming, wanting so intensely to hear the cry, that it is heavy on your mind. Both of these should go away over time. Talk about it. You are not the only one.

Often I felt my baby kicking...this is sometimes called phantom kicking. At first I thought that was very strange and I worried about my sanity. Yet, after a while, and after talking with other mothers, I found that this was common, and I was relieved. Then instead of being afraid of these sensations, I tried to associate them with joyful memories. I didnít hear crying at night, but many mothers have shared that they did.

I still look pregnant. That is too hard to handle.

If your baby died in utero or shortly after birth, you still might look pregnant even weeks after the baby has died. It is likely that people will ask you when your baby is due. Your reactions will depend on the circumstances and your mood at the time. Some days you will be able to respond directly without a lot of anguish, and other days you might not even be able to answer. The emotional and hormonal transitions you are experiencing will take time. Be aware that your reactions will be unpredictable. Allow yourself to feel whatever emotion is within you.

Your body adjusts slowly to not being pregnant any longer. It is unfair and cruel that your body and mind take so long to accomplish this. Try to accept that the changes happen over time. Be patient with yourself.

You might feel the hard part in this situation is that you have made such a sacrifice with your body and 'don't have anything to show for it.' You did have a baby, even if s/he did not live or live long, and now you will have to be patient while you get back in shape. You will find it takes many months to recover physically. You will be happier with yourself if you work on it conscientiously and with patience.

I do remember being upset that my body was such a wreck and I didn't even have a baby to make the sacrifice seem worth it. It seemed unmercifully cruel. About a month after I gave birth, someone in a store asked me when my baby was due. The color rose in my cheeks and I remember stuttering, not knowing what to say. Finally, I decided to tell the truth and not make up a story, as I was tempted to do. The woman seemed genuinely sad; she felt bad that she had asked. Once she was over the shock, we talked about Brennan, what it was like to experience my baby's death, and how I was doing. I was glad I had been able to discuss it with her. On other days, however, there was no way I could tell people the whole story, so I would say I already had my baby and walk away.

What do I have to live for now? Sometimes I feel like I want to die.

The question you are asking is a valid one. What do you have to live for? It probably feels as if your world has collapsed and not much else matters. So maybe you sometimes feel, "I should just give up."

It is very important that you find at least a reason or two to continue living. If you have a reason cemented in your mind, it will act as a buffer and will help you when the urge to 'give up' arises.

You have much to live for if you really think about it and look at your whole life. Sometimes, when in the depths of despair, it is not easy to remember what is good in your life. Your partner, family, friends, clergy, a social worker, or other professional therapist can help you find those reasons, which make your life meaningful. Be aware that not every professional has expertise in every problem, however. If your needs are not being met by your therapist or another professional, or if you do not feel satisfied with the help you are receiving, find someone else. Know that there is someone who can provide valuable assistance for you. You might have to keep looking until you find the appropriate professional.

To work your way out of the depression and the feelings of giving up, think about what you have to look forward to tomorrow or next week. Maybe it is another child's birthday or Confirmation, a vacation or your anniversary, or a project you need to complete. Take it a day at a time, and remind yourself how important you are to others and they are to you. Be aware that thoughts of escaping through sleep, or not wanting to leave the house, or just needing to get away are relatively common at this time.

Many bereaved parents say, "I wish I would have died instead of my child," These feelings usually do not last, but it is a heavy burden to carry alone. Talk it out or write it down. Express your emotions, and do not worry if you feel you are losing it sometimes. It helps to let out your anger and emotions when you are feeling them; when emotions are kept buried they build up to an intensity that sometimes can lead to extreme actions.

Seek help immediately if you feel you cannot resolve your grief on your own or if you feel exceptionally depressed or suicidal, especially if you have a plan to hurt yourself or others. There are many people who care and can be of assistance. Call a social worker, a grief counselor, your clergy, a crisis

intervention line, your local mental health center, or the police immediately.

I don't remember having feelings of wanting to die. It is possible that I did, but maybe I have blocked them out of my thoughts. On most days I knew there were many reasons why I wanted to live and that I did have some things to look forward to, even if a major piece of my life was no longer there. Yet, I do remember having trouble getting up many mornings and wanting to go to sleep for a year, hoping it would be much better then. Some days were harder than others. About six months after Brennan's death I hit rock bottom. It seemed almost worse than when it first happened. Luckily, I was reassured that this was normal and this too would probably pass soon. Feelings like that came and went over the following months. They were less frequent and not so intense over time.

I feel so sad, sometimes I wonder if this healthy?

Actually, experience and studies indicate that stress causes illness. While it is natural to feel sad, depressed, and generally low after such a tragedy, staying there for too long may add to your pain and problems. Indeed, there are many people who believe that when we are down our energy, thoughts, and demeanor can drag us down even lower, negatively affecting ourselves and those around us. And the same goes for being in an upbeat place surrounded by optimistic, positive people. Many who understand kinesiology and Eastern medicine believe that even simple things like a frown or negative thoughts seem to block healthy energy flow in your body, where a simple smile or nice thought brings strength.

Think about it. If someone is in a happy mood, it can be contagious despite your efforts to the contrary. And if they are angry or frustrated, it is easy to go there yourself—at least before this tragedy you might have agreed with this. Maybe a mind in motion with sad thoughts stays in that motion creating more sadness; maybe a mind in motion with positive, hopeful thoughts helps create more positivity and improved health.

This understudied idea may help you. When you are in a dark place wishing you could feel better, smile and think about the good memories and the love you have for your child, or watch a funny movie. Focus on the light side and do something productive or fun… even if part of you does not want to do this now. Take note of how you feel. Relish that respite from sadness. You deserve and need good health and the energy to move forward in your living. The question is, are you ready for it? Can you realize that you still love, honor, and remember your baby without being in anguish all the time.

Bereaved mom, Victoria, suggests that seeking some gratefulness can be helpful when you are ready. Not too long after her eleven-day-old son Isaac died from Trisomy 18, she noticed that she had some feelings of gratefulness. "He had lived for eleven days. Other parents didn't even have that, there was a cause, which many families never learn, we tube fed him, so he didn't have to die from starvation or dehydration unlike if he had been born in an earlier time or remote place without NICU practices available to care for Isaac. He knew the comfort of a nice full baby belly."

Charmayne writes after reading my book, "It felt like Sherokee was sitting beside me talking to me and telling me I was not alone, and I would be okay. I am so very grateful for the impact her words had in my life. After crying myself hoarse, I decided that the only way I was going to make it through this tragedy was to put my broken heart on hold (for a moment), and let my head talk. I am a big believer in your heart has no brains, just emotion, so look at this tragedy with your brain not just your heart!! It was at this point that I realized that there was absolutely nothing that I could do about losing Bryce. He is my baby that just was never meant to be! Crying was not going to change any of this! Feeling sorry for myself, was not going to change it! I had two children who needed their mom, who needed me to be *me*, not the empty shell whose son had died. From that point on I told myself, "There is nothing that I can do to change anything that has happened. I must accept all of this for what it is—the biggest tragedy that I have ever experienced! I must start picking up the pieces of my life and live them. **It is what it is! Nothing is going to change it. So accept it, Charmayne, and move forward!!**"

You may find this style of grieving very helpful when you are able to get there. Acceptance does not mean you won't miss your baby or won't have some sad times. Rather, with this philosophy you may be able to go with the flow a bit more and attempt to see the now and the future. Not everyone will be able to embrace this; however, you may find it works for you, even some of the time.

How will people react toward me now?

You definitely will experience mixed reactions from others. Before your baby was ever born, you had plans and dreams for his or her future as a loved member of your family. S/he existed as a real, special, and unique person...one no one really knew, or barely knew, as well as you did. You grieve for that baby as a real member of your family. You grieve for the future with him or her that can no longer be.

Though they want to comfort and support you, most family and friends probably will not have the same intensity about this loss as you. Surely they will feel some sadness. The death of an infant is most unusual and difficult for people. Maybe they never or hardly met, held, or played with your baby. They did not spend as many hours as you did thinking about what the baby would look like and dreaming about this baby as a member of the family. Or they spent little time with your baby who lived for a while and may think that having a baby die early is easier than a two or three-year-old. For any number of reasons, mainly they will experience the grief through you. They hurt mostly because you hurt. Help them to know what would be of benefit to you.

On the other hand, close family, and friends who have been excited and felt interested may be so hurt and full of sorrow that they have little energy to help you much. Grandparents seem to have a double loss–the loss of their precious grandchild and the realization that they cannot take your pain away. Relatives and friends might really want to help but struggle with how to do that. They may even say things that hurt more than help. They are coping in the best way they know how right now. Probably this is how they have handled their own personal crises in the past and when hurt again they are almost on automatic pilot. Try to be patient and not judge them. Give them time.

You might find that some well-meaning people believe that since your baby did not live, or did not live very long, your attachment is less than if you had a two-year-old or a 20-year-old. This is not true, although each loss if different and unique. When your hopes, dreams, and the very real attachment came to an end after months or years of anticipation, the grief can be extremely intense. As one mother put it, "On a scale of one to ten, when your child dies, it is always a ten." So, no matter when your baby died; three months in utero, at birth or after birth, you have every right to feel sad, angry, lonely, and more.

Other people's reactions to your news will be varied. Sometimes even close friends and family members might avoid you or the subject of your baby's death. They probably do not realize your need to talk. Or they might say things that seem trivial or very painful to you. For example, someone might tell you, "You didn't really know her anyway," or "At least you have other children," or " You can always have another baby." They say these things because they do not want you to hurt any more than you already do. Many people have difficulty talking about death and knowing how to comfort the survivors. If possible help them understand that you are hurting and you have the right to feel such pain. When you love someone and they die, does it really matter how long you have known them? Can one quantify the amount of love one holds for another by the months or years you have known them? Or do you grieve as deeply as you grieve because you simply love them and now they are gone?

Some Things You Can Do That Might Help

When you are ready, here are some suggestions of things you can do that might aid you in getting through some of the tough days:

- Involve your family and friends immediately to share your grief and to gain their support. Use their strength and let them help. Support is one of the first and most important things you will need.

- When they ask what they can do to help, give specific suggestions. Tell them you need food, company, childcare, prayer, help driving, etc. Give them this book to read. They want to do something, so help them to know what you need. It is not easy to admit or ask for help. This takes courage, but it can diminish your pain and loneliness.

- Good nutrition is the next most important thing you will need. If you can't think much about food at the time, ask someone to help you. Well-balanced meals will help your body and mind recover. Drink lots of fluids, water, and juice mostly. This cleanses the body of toxins and helps you regain your health.

- Try to stay away from, or cut down on, alcohol or medication such as tranquilizers or sleeping pills. They tend to dull the senses and protect you from the harsh reality. But once you stop or take a break, reality sets in maybe harder then before. They may temporarily ease physical and emotional pain but you may pay a price for this with side effects. Speak with your medical care provider about this if you have concerns.

- Get plenty of regular rest, even if you can't sleep. Try to stay on a schedule, which is what your body needs now.

- Be active, exercise, walk; and do something physical. It helps to release some of the anger and frustration and also is good for recovering.

- Go out in the sunshine (or use a full spectrum light bulb if it is winter.) It is healing and the production of vitamin D is critical to help the body use vitamins and minerals and heal. Vitamin C is good to boost the immune system, which is probably low due to the stress.

- It is common to find your mind wandering; you should not operate heavy or dangerous equipment, including driving a car during extremely stressful times. Many people have commented that they have no idea how they got to their destination. They hardly remember driving, yet they did. Be careful. This puts your life in danger, as well as endangering other innocent people. Ask for a ride and take time off work for a while if you do operate dangerous equipment.

- Talk or write about your baby, your feelings, and your grief with your partner, family, friends, co-workers, and other bereaved parents. This will not go away just because you ignore it or try to forget it.

- When you talk about your baby, use his or her name, which makes your baby more real recognizing the importance of this person in your life.

- Talk about the delivery, the death, how s/he looked, your fears, any happiness, apprehension, or despair you felt. If you have pictures, show them to others, if you choose to do so.

- Acknowledge your parenthood, even if this was your first child. Remember, you are a parent. Life will never be quite the same as before. Believe you will find a new normal someday.

- Share the first days at home together with your partner. If dad can take some time off from work, make a point to do it so you will have those hours with each other.

- Encourage visitors when ready. This might help lessen some of the emptiness you probably feel and can keep you involved in the world.

- You may notice an inability to make decisions, accomplish even normal things, and even a difficulty in getting out of bed. Your priorities may change and you might not know how to deal with this. Keep in mind that this is only a temporary 'you.' It is what happens to many people during grief. Don't fight it too hard, and recognize that this is normal.

- Mom, it is likely that you may remain at home for a while if you are recovering from a birth. Emotionally you may feel better if you are involved with work, a hobby, or community activities when you feel ready. Don't become so busy, however, that you avoid thinking about your loss and grief totally.

- Avoid making hasty decisions about the baby's belongings and room. Do not let others take over or make decisions for you. This is part of your process. You should choose whether to put things away or leave them out. Whatever you decide, use this time, as difficult and painful as it will be, to share tears, unmet dreams, and stories of the pregnancy.

- Write your feelings down in a journal. Make a baby book with mementos, cards, keepsakes, etc. You can keep the memory of your baby alive with such things as a framed poem that was special to you, a set of footprints, baby pictures, or some other special items.

- Talk to your clergy or spiritual advisor to help you understand and deal with or restore your faith in God if you find it failing.

- Set time aside periodically (daily, and then weekly, as time progresses) to talk with your partner. Time will pass, but still you will feel a need to talk about your baby and your grief.

- Since this time is stressful, try not to make major changes in your life, such as job changes, moving, or a permanent decision regarding more children. Keep as much of the rest of your life as intact as you can.

- Read books articles, and poems (see **Bibliography**), to help you understand and to seek comfort so you will not feel so alone.

- Call local hospitals or national support organizations (listed in **Resources**) to find support people or a group that specifically helps parents whose baby has died. This will give you an opportunity to talk with others who have 'been there;' others who can offer you support and hope. The internet has many, many websites that will help.

AFTER
SOME TIME
HAS PASSED

Some days you will feel as if you are well on the road to recovery, and on others you will feel as if you are right back in the middle of all that grief. One mother commented that she felt she would 'move one step ahead, then two steps backward.' You will find this to be a very up and down emotional period. A song, a diaper commercial, the grocery aisles, or any event or place has the potential to set you off. That is very normal, and try as you will, rarely can it be controlled.

Trust and believe that it can get better over time and with much work. Though it may be hard to believe some days, the pain does lessen, although it might never go away completely. Ask yourself, when you love someone so deeply is it even right to think that you should get over them quickly and never have painful reminders? Aren't they worth remembering and yes, occasionally crying over, even years later? In time you will find that bittersweet memories can never poison their preciousness in your heart and mind. Those are the feelings and memories that will sustain you over time.

As you come to cope and adapt from day to day, week to week, and eventually month to month you will begin to accept your baby's death and learn to live again. Probably s/he is in your thoughts often and surely will always be a member of your family. In fact, many people describe their relationship as one of still being a parent to this child who has died, a very healthy philosophy. They may decorate the grave on every holiday and special day, buy presents in memory of their baby, donate toys to a charity, celebrate his or her birthday with a cake and balloons, and include him or her in their family when talking with others. All of these things can be part of the healing process. In fact, there may be many days when you feel pride and even joy that your child existed, and you are thankful for the changes his or her short life has made in you and others.

All of this is not to say you still won't be angry or frustrated at times. You will continue to miss your baby and all that 'could have been.' It is quite common to feel cheated that you are not spending time parenting this child instead of grieving or trying to keep busy in other ways.

When I first wrote this section, eight months after Brennan's death it seemed that hardly a day went by when I didn't think about Brennan or this tragic experience. I wrote, "At least now I do not fall to pieces every time I think about him. I have talked about him so much that my emotions usually do not jump out and take over every time. But sometimes they do, and I cannot stop that. I try to go with the flow and trust my body and my heart. Brennan's memory has faded some, but the love I will always feel for him reminds me that he is worth loving and remembering. He is someone I will never forget."

Now, years later, mostly I smile with pride when I think of Brennan, Marama, and Bryna. They would be so proud of their loving family, and we are so thankful to them for the impact their short lives have made on us. Yes, there are days when we wish they were here, on earth, but mostly we deal well with their place in our lives and our hearts. We enjoy talking about them sometimes, wondering such things as what they would be like and what gifts we would give them on their birthdays if they were alive.

I am fearful of having sexual intercourse with my partner. Somehow this doesn't seem right.

Sexuality is an issue that is rarely discussed openly after a healthy baby is born and even less so when a baby dies. But it should be talked about. It might seem healthy and normal for you to have sexual intercourse and be intimately close at this time. Or one or both of you might have a difficult time feeling comfortable about lovemaking after the death of your baby. In your mind, you might link the act of intercourse with the conception and therefore, the death of your baby. You might feel guilty or angry that this was the 'beginning or cause of this tragedy and all my pain.' Though this is very common, this could be a problem for your relationship if it goes on too long and probably should be talked out.

Maybe it will not be easy for you to enjoy sex or intimacy if you feel you should be in mourning and not thinking about yourself. Try not to feel guilty about any more things in your life than you already do. If you can keep thoughts of the baby out of the bedroom, more power to you. If not, try to work this out so it doesn't keep you apart. More than ever, you need each other now. Being close and intimate could aid in your recovery. You deserve and need some private and warm time together. If one of you does not feel comfortable, do take things slowly. Maybe in the beginning you can caress and cuddle as a first step while you continually keep the lines of communication open. Try to be patient with yourself and your partner.

Free yourself to seek professional help at any time as you struggle to cope and survive. A trained counselor may be able to help you listen to each other and work through the tough issues.

There were some fearful feelings about lovemaking for me, and then other times I looked forward to the intimacy of it. This was one of the few times when thoughts of Brennan didn't overpower all my other thoughts. However, I must admit that there were those times when tears would flow and memories surfaced. We both tried to talk through this. The closeness and private time was most comforting to both of us.

My friends, family and co-workers seem to have forgotten we ever had this baby. No one ever asks about him or her.

After awhile, sometimes no longer than a month, people will stop bringing up the subject of your baby. They might feel you are 'over it' by now or just want to protect you from those painful memories. They might believe that if they bring it up they will hurt you and make you cry. If you need to talk about it with them, you most likely will have to be the strong and assertive one to bring it up. Though this doesn't seem fair; people are often waiting for your cues. Let people know that you are not trying to forget your baby but want to remember. Ask them to say your baby's name out loud, to be prepared that anniversaries and holidays will be hard, and to help include this child as a family member. The sooner you do this, the easier and more accepted this will be within your family.

I felt badly when people stopped asking me about Brennan and how I was doing. After not talking about it much, sometimes I wondered if I ever really had been pregnant or had a baby. My body had recovered and did not look pregnant. I had little around the house to remind me of Brennan. On those days when I questioned if I had a baby, I needed to feel that pain, to remember, and to talk about him. On a rare occasion, I would get up enough nerve to call a relative or friend and either hint or directly bring forth those memories. The memories, the pain, and after a while the joy I also felt, were like jolts reminding me that yes, it was true; I was a mother. I had a child. And love lasts forever.

People ask me how many children I have? How do I answer this?

Everyone will answer this slightly differently, but the main issue seems to be—do you mention your child(ren) who have died or only those who live? If there are no living children do you say *none*?

Be true to yourself, and know when you have strength and energy to 'take this on.' You surely have the right to include the children who have died as members of your family. Some people comment that they feel terrible if they leave out the child who has died. Yet, if they bring it up, people will feel uncomfortable and stumble over their words. Is it right to protect people from feeling uncomfortable while sacrificing your own needs? Sometimes yes, sometimes no. Each time, you will have to decide.

It may be that you don't have the time to go into it, so you choose not to bring it up. Other times you may feel like talking about it and bringing others into the reality of life, your life at least. Its okay to go back and forth as long as you know in your own heart how many children you have. When a 20-year-old dies are they no longer a member of the family, a son or daughter? Of course they are! Their picture usually remains on the wall and though they are not talked about every day, they are forever a brother, a sister, a son, or daughter.

Try out different responses and find which ones you feel the most comfortable with. Have an answer ready because you will be asked this question. Just don't go against your own wishes in order to make it easy for others. If we don't talk about this and show people that we can survive and that we need help, how will they ever learn? It is not our place to protect them, but rather we can include them and sometimes even teach them.

When someone asks me how many children I have, there are a few responses I give. One is, "I have five children, two are living and three in heaven." Or I might say, "Two living." That then leaves the door open if they want to go further. Often people do. I also must admit there are days lately when I merely say, 'Two." It is just easier and I don't have time or energy to go into it.

Holidays, anniversaries and birthdays are hard.

In the beginning, the day of the week and the hour your baby died will be the times you dread. You may notice that you measure time in those periods. After awhile the anniversary date in each month will have significance. Later it will stretch out to other dates such as due dates, holidays, and anniversaries. These can be difficult times for you. The anticipation is usually worse than the actual day. The best thing you can do is to decide for yourself what you want to happen on those days. For instance, you may want cards and flowers on Mother's Day, though you have no living children. Or you may want to light candles on Christmas or Hanukkah in memory of your child. Or you may want to leave town this year and change the typical celebration so it doesn't hurt so much. Whatever you feel you need to do, be direct with others so they can help you in achieving this. Tell a few people you hope to receive a Mother's/Father's Day card, ask family to understand why you need to get away this year, or tell them a few weeks before the one year anniversary of the death that it is coming up which can help them remember. Asking for help is the one thing that is likely to aid you the most. Try to make yourself do this. Believe that someone will come through for you.

Many people remembered us on Brennan's first birthday with cards, plants, flowers, a locket, their presence, and prayers. We appreciated this more than anyone will ever know. Each anniversary and holiday was difficult for a long while. Mother's and Father's Days were among the hardest, even after we had a living child. There were disappointments with how people handled it, and we often understood that they didn't know how to approach us or what to say. Thankfully, we had each other to respond to our wishes, though we weren't always on the same wavelength. Nor did we have the same needs. In those cases, when I needed to do something (like go to the hospital on Brennan's one year anniversary and re-experience his birth and death), I sought out a friend I knew would encourage and support me.

Now, years later, we celebrate Brennan's birthday with our living children by making a cake, singing to him and trying to imagine what he would be like (probably teasing his younger brothers) and what toys he might like (a skateboard or scooter?) It has become a special and mostly upbeat day. When we get a card or call from a friend it makes it extra special. Though we don't need that as we did in the early years, we appreciate them for remembering and reaching out.

Are there any special memorial events or activities to honor babies?

In fact, there are many activities throughout the US, Australia, Canada, UK, New Zealand, and many other countries, especially near Mother and Father's Day, holidays, and in quite a few places due to October being declared Pregnancy and Infant Loss Awareness Month (this includes miscarriage, stillbirth, neonatal death, SIDS, and other infant deaths.) I know about this unified effort because I led a team of national organizations including SHARE and RTS to seek a Presidential Proclamation in 1988 in the US, and as a board member of ISA we are working to keep a list of all events on the site – www.pregnancyandinfantloss.com. Events are led by individuals, support groups, hospitals, and organizations and include such activities as Walks to Remember, memorial services, dinners, auctions, training programs for professionals, special support group meetings with speakers, and so much more. Check it out and think about attending; it will be a wonderful way to meet others and to remember your baby.

What about having another baby?

Books are written on this question alone. In fact, I have written one, _Another Baby? Maybe..._Other popular ones are _Still to be Born_ and _When Pregnancy Follows Loss._ This is an important question and needs to be covered here, too. Maybe you are one of the many people trying for another baby soon after the loss. It is natural that you want to fill your empty arms. You have room in your home and your heart for a baby. Yet, you may feel frightened at what could happen next time.

It's also unfair to have to wait and go through this all again. If you had infertility problems or other losses, it may seem especially cruel. Be a little careful about quickly jumping into another pregnancy. You will need to figure out how long to wait and what seems right for you.

If you can wait for a little while, you can do some of the heavier grief work, which may lighten the load and help you become more emotionally healthy during a subsequent pregnancy. Another baby does not make it all better. If you do end up pregnant soon, you will handle that as well as you can, so don't fret or worry about it. For many parents, the thought of having another baby brings comfort, even if not right now. Others comment that they feel they are betraying their baby who has died. The 'right' time to embark on this will vary depending on your individual circumstances. Trust yourself about that timing; just don't rush to do this right away. Experts and most parents agree that working through some of your grief before having another baby might help you from trying to 'replace' the one who died. It also may help you be a little more calm and hopeful during another pregnancy if you've worked through some of your grief. The creation of a new life can provide an opportunity for another beginning.

When you are pregnant again, assuming you have few problems, you may find you have to get past the point of your last loss before you feel hopeful and calm. Some people admit never feeling calm until they have their live baby in their arms or maybe even until the child is a year old, past the fear of when SIDS eases. The pregnancy can seem to last forever, and it may be hard not to believe that *it* won't happen again. In a way, your protective bubble, your innocence, has been burst and you may now feel very vulnerable.

Kick counting is becoming a recommended practice to help moms be more aware of the baby's movement. When significant changes take place from the baby's normal pattern, calling a doctor immediately is advised. To learn more about kick counting visit the website www.babykickalliance.org or www.stillnomore.org.

When and if it comes to thinking about parenting another baby, you may find yourself feeling overprotective and fearful. That can occur with your surviving children even now. You know that tragedy can strike, at any time because you have experienced it, and naturally you wish to do what you can to protect your other children. In the case of a surviving twin, you will be frightened that the same thing could happen. This will be a very anxious time. As with other child losses, marriages and relationships are easily strained and stressed, especially if there are any doubts or feelings of blame. You will need to work at not being too overprotective and at staying close as a couple. Both are challenges, but this is possible. Make a commitment, then work at it.

Ask your medical caregiver for extra tests and reassurance as often as you need it. You are paying for your health care; they are working for you, and this is your only chance with this particular child and this pregnancy. Be an advocate for yourself, ask questions, call when you are concerned, and seek second opinions when you need more information to make a decision.

Building a good support system during subsequent pregnancies can really help. There may be a pregnancy loss and infant death support group in your area. Often they have pregnant members in the same situation. Or maybe you can find another parent who is pregnant again after a loss or who has had another baby. Search within your community for people who will listen to your fears, not give you unsolicited advice or assure you that everything will be okay. Your fears are real and you know better than others that there are no guarantees that everything will be okay. Seek people who will be with you when you need them.

Try to be hopeful, as difficult as that may be. It may be especially hard if you have had more than one loss. Nancy, a mother who had experienced five losses, had an interesting philosophy that I have come to admire. She felt that her energy during each subsequent pregnancy ought to be directed toward the tiny living baby within her. Instead of being afraid of bonding and feeling hopeless, she talked and sang often to her baby, made positive plans for the future, and tried to let that child know that s/he was loved and wanted. Her reasoning was, "If I only get three weeks or a few months with this baby before s/he is miscarried or dies, I want to feel good about what I did, not guilty. I want to build special memories of whatever time we have together, because I will need that if something bad happens. And if everything turns out fine I will be thankful for all of that special time and won't have regrets either."

During our subsequent pregnancy with Kellan, who was born a year and three months after Brennan, we were both nervous wrecks. We describe that as the 'world's longest pregnancy.' I thought I would never make it to the end with a healthy baby. People would ask, "When is your baby due?" and I could only answer, "If everything goes okay, in February." Never could I just say, 'February.' That sounded like a guarantee and I knew I had none. People would say to us, "Well, think positive; it just can't happen again." To this I would reply, "Will you make me a promise? Can you put that in writing?" I knew all too well that if it happened to us once, nothing made us so special that it wouldn't happen again.

Thankfully, Kellan was born three weeks early and very healthy. With his birth cry, I felt a heavy weight suddenly lift from my shoulders and heart. What a relief! My sensitive medical caregivers asked if he looked like Brennan and wondered how the two labors and births compared. When Trevor was born two years later, the fear and release of anxiety at his birth were very similar to Kellan's. I guess even having a living child hadn't taken away my feelings of vulnerability.

I must admit that often when I held each baby, usually at night, I felt fearful that they, too, would die. Many nights after Kellan was born I was convinced he had died, and I would plan his funeral in my mind. Even now, sometimes I look at both boys and wonder how long I will have them with me on earth. No longer can I take birth and a long life as a given. Life is fragile, and if we dare to love, we dare to lose. Maybe that makes those I love more precious to me. I rarely take them for granted.

What if this loss might be the last baby?

If you have experienced previous infertility, or have been told this is your last pregnancy, or have made that decision reluctantly, you may feel frustrated. The pregnancy that ended tragically may have symbolized a miracle, a once in a lifetime chance for parenthood. If this is the case for you, the loss is twofold. There is the loss of the baby and this death compounds the loss of self-esteem that goes hand-in-hand with the difficulty in conceiving and/or carrying a baby to term. You may feel particularly isolated, since such a tragedy often results in a withdrawal from friends and relatives with children. Even if you have other children you may not want to end on this note. If your family plan included more children and that is no longer an option, it may be a very difficult. This is another loss, the loss of any more biological children you might have wanted, though maybe you wish to consider adoption at some point.

Well-meaning friends and relatives may actually add to the pain after your loss by making comments such as, "Well, you can try again," not knowing your circumstances. Or they may suggest, "You can always adopt." It may be that you can't 'just adopt.' Adoption is a long process, with waiting lists of many years and is very expensive. The death of a baby is a terrible thing for anyone to bear. It is no easier even if you might be able to have other children.

What can I do to move on in a healthy manner?

- Realize that you are dealing with this loss and moving forward. You are doing what you can.

- Treat yourself to something special—a dinner out, a new outfit, a special tool you may have been wanting, a trip, or a vacation.

- Continue to exercise, working off your frustrations, along with getting yourself in shape. It is good for your physical and mental health.

- When considering especially painful activities, put your needs first. If there are baptisms and baby showers, you may feel pressure, from yourself and others, to go and be happy for them. If you really can't go or just don't think it will be good for you, then don't. Later you may feel more ready and you will know when the time is right. You might want to ask a close loved one to pass on to others, if appropriate, that you need to protect yourself right now. Though you really are happy for this family, it hurts too much and reminds you of what you don't have. Be honest. Most people will be understanding.

- Try some fun activities and be open to talk about 'other things,' when you seem ready, even if it seems impossible. You will probably find that those other things now are talked about in the light of the loss. Things are different now, and for most people, the loss cannot be denied. While it might have been hard to put it away for a night, that will change eventually, naturally, and doesn't have to be forced, especially by others. Do work to bring even minutes or hours of happiness and humor back into your life. Do not feel guilty for laughing or desiring happiness. After all you have been through, you deserve to balance all the sadness and sorrow.

- Try writing a letter or keep a journal of your letters to your baby. Many parents and grandparents have found this very helpful and therapeutic. Say all the things you wanted to say but didn't get to.

- Write letters, even if you never send them, to the people or care providers who you are dissatisfied with or who really helped you. If you can send the letters it might be enlightening information for these people. They may appreciate hearing their successes as well as where they could improve. Of course, not all will take criticism easily. Even if you don't send the letters you may feel better just writing them and getting it out of your mind.

- Be aware that holidays, birthdays, death dates, and due dates can be very sad, lonely, and trying times. It is common for the anticipation of these difficult days to be worse than the actual day, especially if you take charge and make some plans for the day. The dread and fear can be quite draining. Some of the more difficult periods seem to be one month, five to six months, and one year after the death of your child. But each person is unique and the tough times can come at any point and do not follow a schedule. Many situations can trigger memories, such as seeing other babies, baptisms, baby showers and other pregnant women.

GAINING PERSPECTIVE AND FINDING HOPE

Even though you want to hear, and believe, that you will recover quickly and completely from the death of your child, that is rarely the case. It is a very complex process that takes time and much work, after all grieving so hard is a testament to the amount of your love. Healing, gaining perspective, and finding hope are different for everyone. For you, it might mean less frequent crying, making it through days feeling somewhat normal, or remembering your baby without so much anguish. Or it might mean laughing and smiling often. Or it may mean being able to concentrate on work again or trying for another baby. Maybe you will return to other activities as you reconstruct your life, allowing other things to become important to you again.

Some of the pain might always be with you, as will the memory of your son or daughter. Continually try to express your sadness, anger, and other feelings and to fondly, warmly, and lovingly remember your baby. One mother wisely stated that, "Once I knew it was all right to admit to the pain and to know that I would always love my daughter who had died, I started to feel better." You never have to stop loving your child.

Other people often give the message: "Now that it has been a year, you should be over it." Sometimes they say that after only a few months. Let them know you still have bad times, but yes, you also have good times. People who have experienced a death themselves understand this.

There is no magic date, such as a one or ten year anniversary, when you will feel instantly healed. Just because many months or years have passed, do not expect that the bad days are all over for you. It is a lifelong process. Most of the hurt probably will lessen, but there still will be days when you are overcome by sadness. Allow that to happen.

Two women, one 85 and the other 97, each gave birth to many children, several who lived, and both had a baby who died. Their eyes well up with tears when they talk about their son or daughter and what their child might have been like today.

EMPTY ARMS

When I first wrote this book I stated, "I do believe that now, eight months later, I am well on my way to feeling recovered. There are many people and activities that once again are important to me. I feel that Brennan's death is in perspective with the rest of my life. When I remember him, I still am deeply saddened. I will never forget, and I know the pain won't ever go away completely. But I do have happiness in my life, and I have many good days."

Now, many years later, I rarely feel the deep sadness and sorrow as in the early days. Most of the time I am caught up in other life activities. There are many times when I can hardly remember how devastated I felt at the time. It, too, has faded in my memory. My love for all my children brings me many smiles, much pride, and tears only some of the time. Though their lives have been short, the gifts they each have given our whole family are immeasurable. For that we all are grateful.

I found comfort in the following poem by Abraham Lincoln, who had three sons who died—Edward, 4, William, 11, and Thomas, 18.

> In this sad world of ours, sorrow comes to all...
> It comes with bitterest agony...
> Perfect relief is not possible, except with time.
> You cannot now realize that you will ever feel better...
> And yet this is a mistake.
> You are sure to be happy again.
> To know this, which is certainly true,
> Will make you become less miserable now.
> I have experienced enough to know what I say.

I also found great comfort and encouragement to risk and to dare to love again from this quote by Earl Grollman in his book <u>Time Remembered.</u>

> It is a risk to attempt new beginnings.
> Yet the greater risk is for you to risk nothing.
> For there will be no further possibilities
> of learning and changing,
> of traveling upon the journey of life.
> You were strong to hold on.
> You will be stronger to go forward to new beginnings.

May you dare to risk your love again and again as you travel the journey of life. Stay strong, go forward, and seek new beginnings when you must.

Hope...Time...Love...Healing

Tomorrow will come. The pain will ease. But you will never forget your precious child. It takes hope and time and love for the healing to take place. Remember along the way to accept, but never, ever forget.

WHAT FAMILY AND FRIENDS CAN DO

Loved ones, this is for you. It is not easy to know what to do or say to someone whose baby has died. Death reminds us all of our own humanness and mortality. Most of us would rather not think or talk about death. However, at this painful time in the parent's lives, they need to talk about their baby, their feelings, and their concerns. It seems unreal to have to deal with the death of a baby. All were waiting for the joyous day and now the opposite has happened. Or you had celebrated new life and then the baby died.

Friends and family can aid and support the parents by encouraging them to talk and by remembering and honoring the baby. This helps them to face the death and grieve themselves, along with sharing this intense pain with you. Ignoring the subject does not make it go away, nor does it make the parents feel less pain. Don't protect them from this pain. Instead help them face it. In most cases, it hurts more when people will not talk about it with the parents. This is often interpreted by parents as insensitivity, disinterest, or a minimization of the loss of their child. They need to know that you, their loved ones, are willing and interested in hearing about their experience. After all, this has probably been the most tragic and devastating event in their lives. They had a baby and now that baby has died. They will always be parents of this child, and you will always be related and/or connected to this child, too. Get involved, stay tuned in, respect their wishes, and realize that you also have experienced a loss and will need to do your own grief work.

What can I do to help the parents?

- Offer a tear, a hug, a sign of love and concern.

- Listen; then talk about the death and about their son or daughter. Ask questions if they want to talk. Most parents need and want to talk about their baby, their hopes and dreams with their child that has died, even if it was a miscarriage. Ask the parents, "Do you feel like talking about it now or would later be better?"

- Realize that the parents are sad because they miss this baby, this special person; he or she never can be replaced by anyone else. They had pictured their child in their minds, learning to walk, starting school, making friends, graduating, getting married and having their own children. This was not 'just' a baby but a real person and a whole future that has been lost.

- Say the baby's name out loud and often if s/he has been named. This special child deserves to be remembered and saying his or her name is very affirming to the parents.

- Comments such as, "I am sorry about your sweet baby," or "I know this is a bad time for you, and I would like to help," or "Please tell me what you would like me to do," or "Can I bring dinner over?" and "I feel so sad," might seem trite, but they really do help.

- Comments such as "It was for the best," "It might have been abnormal," "You can always have another baby," "Forget it, put it behind you," tend to deny the importance of this baby in the parent's lives.

- Send a card, note, poem, or some other personal expression of sympathy after the death, especially after a few weeks. Most cards stop coming then, and that's when the shock seems to set in. Also remember anniversaries, holidays, and due dates with a card, call or visit.

- Bring a dish of healthy food to the family, especially after a few weeks have passed. This is when their reality sets in and few people come around. Cooking will still be unimportant, yet eating nutritionally is critical to regain health.

- Offer to baby-sit the other children, wash clothes, or do some other household chores.

- Bring a book that might offer comfort or some understanding (see **Bibliography** for suggestions).

- Give a gift certificate for a dinner or maybe a facial or massage at the local spa or health club. Massages can be most helpful since the body is so tense during this difficult time.

- Give a plant, a living bush, a tree, or flowers. Sometimes living things represent continuity and a sense of future, which is so desperately needed at this time. When they bloom they will be beautiful reminders of the love you and the parents have for their child.

- Pass on names and phone numbers of others who have experienced a similar loss and seem to be coping well. There is a real need to talk with others who 'have been through it.' Offer to make the call for them, since it is very difficult to call someone you don't know when you are hurting.

- Ask parents about their preference regarding donating money and memorials. I used the donated money to help publish this book.

- Search the internet or call your local hospital to learn about support groups in the area or the many pregnancy and infant loss activities such as memorial services, Walks to Remember, and fundraising events that occur especially in October in the US, UK, Canada, New Zealand, and Australia as well as close to holidays. Attending such events can mean so much to you, your family, and the parents.

- Recognize the parent's grief and healing process will be painful and will take time, lots of time. They will not be recovered or done 'thinking about, grieving, or remembering their baby' after a month or even a year. Love lasts forever.

- Be aware that never again will they be quite the same people you knew before they had this baby. Their lives have changed; their perspectives and goals will be different. Recognize and respect this. Their goal will be to find a 'new' normal, not their old normal.

- Do not judge them and what they are doing (unless they are physically hurting themselves or others). When a bereaved person is grieving they can look like they are going crazy, but that does not mean they are. It is natural for them to forget things, make statements that seem off the wall or unusual, not keep promises, or seek out comfort in ways that are atypical from their personalities. They are out of control and can't think straight. In time this will change. Your patience, understanding, and support at this time are critical.

- Try to sort out which are your issues and wishes for them and which are not. Sometimes your ideas on how they should be grieving, moving on, or just plain living is not their way of coping. It may not be a 'problem' for them at all, though you may find it uncomfortable.

- Eventually, be willing to discuss other topics besides their loss, since life must go on. But take your cues from them. If they need to stay focused on their process and feelings, they may not be ready to stray too far to other topics as often as you may wish.

- Be prepared that they will probably look at all other life issues in light of this loss. It may be on their minds always, especially in the beginning months.

- Again, recognize the importance of this child. The loss and pain cannot be replaced with another baby. And do make the effort to remember their baby and inquire as to how they are doing. Months down the road a simple "How have you been doing since your baby (say the name) died?" can give much comfort.

- Be patient and be there. They need you now more than ever.

Your assistance, comfort, and support can be very influential in how the parents cope with the death of their baby and how they recover. You are important, dear loved ones; they need you now more than ever. And in order to be of support to others, you will need to make sure your lamp is filled with oil, so you can shine some light. Face your own feelings of loss and take care of yourself, too.

SUPPORT RESOURCES
Organizations
INFANT LOSS

1st Breath Provides education, advocacy, and public awareness of stillbirth. Assists families, trains professionals, and offers support packets to hospitals. www.1stbreath.org

A Place to Remember (800) 631-0973. Sells birth/death announcement, sympathy cards, mementos, and literature on perinatal loss, has online memorial site, extensive resource links. www.aplacetoremember.com MemorEmedia.com offers downloadable books.

Angel Layettes Dedicated to provide comfort, love, dignity and compassion after a baby dies, they provide pretty hand-sewn burial layettes, blankets, sewn hearts, and memorial keepsakes to hospitals at no charge. www.angellayettes.org

Angel Names Association Nonprofit organization that assists families of stillborn children with financial assistance for end-of-life expenses and counseling services and funding for stillbirth research. www.angelnames.org

Baby Loss, An online community offering information and support for bereaved parents who have suffered the death of a baby through miscarriage, ectopic pregnancy, intra-uterine death, stillbirth or other types of pregnancy loss. www.babyloss.com

Babies Remembered (952) 476-1303. Supports and advocates for families, training for professionals, and sells literature and audio-visuals. Sherokee Ilse and Associates consult with facilities and organizations that support families. Offer poems, articles, studies/research, offers updates on infant loss and general bereavement issues. www.BabiesRemembered.org

Baby Loss Family Advisors™ /Baby Loss Doulas® These compassionate, certifying Independent Advocates have extensive training and preparation to support newly bereaved families as early as 'upon hearing the news'. They can help create birth/parenting plans with families for miscarriage or any other child losses, be a navigator/companion during some of the hospital stay, and beyond. This service offers 'shell-shocked' bereaved parents a chance to have a wise guide on the side during the ensuing trauma, helping them to make better decisions about welcoming their baby, eventually saying goodbyes, and re-entry into work and life. A list of BLFA/BLD professionals and certification classes are found at - www.BabyLossFamilyAdvisors.org

Centering Corporation (866) 218-0101. Sells literature on death, dying and coping with bereavement issues, including pregnancy loss, illness, death of children, adults, and pets. www.Centering.org

Center for Loss in Multiple Birth, Inc. (Climb) (907) 222-5321. Support network by-for parents after death of one or more babies from a twin or higher multiple pregnancy/birth. www.climb-support.org

Compassion Books (828) 675-5909. Mail order catalog, resources on grief, death, dying, comfort, and hope. www.compassionbooks.com

Compassionate Friends, Inc. (US Office) (877) 969-0010. A self-help organization for families who experience a death of a child. Newsletter and local support groups www.compassionatefriends.org. Canadian Office www.tcfcanada.net

The Daily Strength Stillbirth Forum Online support group for parents to share feelings including Angel Babies. www.dailystrength/org/c/stillbirth

Faith's Lodge, A place where those coping with the serious illness or death of a child can find hope and strength for the future www.faithslodge.org

Faces of Loss, Faces of Hope Seeks to "put a face" on perinatal loss. Online support community with hundreds of pregnancy/infant loss stories. Searchable-types of loss, stage, date of loss, location, and keywords, blog directory, extensive resource guide, virtual book clubs, gift exchanges, and more. In-person support,Face2Face Friendship Groups program. www.facesofloss.com

First Candle/SIDS Alliance (800) 221-7437. Promotes research on causes and prevention, responds to parents, families, professionals, and the general public seeking information and support on stillbirth and SIDS. Publications and newsletter. www.firstcandle.org

Grieve Out Loud Pen-Pal Program connects babyloss parents, grandparents to others after miscarriage, stillbirth, or infant death. www.grieveoutloud.org

Group B Strep Offer support and information, education, awareness, promotes testing and treatment of GBS. www.groupbstrepinternational.org

Heavenly Angels in Need Offers many different kinds of help to babies, children and their families in need. http://heavenlyangelsinneed.com /HomeMenu.php

Healing Hearts Shop Online shop that has loss-oriented gifts, jewelry, beaded items, books, booklets, A-V, and Loss Doula packets. Created by Sherokee Ilse, accepting consignment artists. www.HealingHeartsShop.com

Innocents Especially for children with no grave or headstone. At The Church of The Holy Innocents, parents are able to name your child(ren) and to have the opportunity to have their baby's name inscribed in our "BOOK OF LIFE" and a candle is always lit in their memory. www.innocents.com/shrine.asp

International Stillbirth Alliance (ISA) International Stillbirth Alliance. Int'l coalition of organizations founded by stillbirth parents; promotes research, raises awareness, educates www.stillbirthalliance.org

International Society for the Study and Prevention of Perinatal and Infant Death (ISPID) Leaders in the world in discovering evidence-based preventative measures for stillbirth and sudden infant death. Promotes education and awareness for families and researchers. www.ispid.org

Mary Madeline Project A non-profit founded in memory of Madeline Marie Erickson who died at seven weeks of age that donates beautiful infant / baby burial gowns and blankets to hospitals for bereaving parents (miscarriage and beyond) made from wedding gowns/prom dresses www.marymadelineproject.org

Missing Grace A web based support system that helps families with pregnancy and infant loss, infertility, and adoption. Support, resources, promote awareness and the prevention of stillbirth. www.missinggrace.org

MISS (Mothers in Sympathy and Support) (623) 979-1000. Helps families after stillbirth, early infant death, or any child through local support groups, camps for grieving kids, resources, newsletters, and web site. Advocay for Missing Angel Bill (certificates of birth in US) www.missfoundation.org

NeoFight (317) 446-3013 (24 hour email helpline). Supports families in perinatal crisis including a difficult pregnancy, miscarriage, stillbirth, neonatal death and premature babies. Also offers training program for parent listeners. www.neofight.org

Parent Support is a group of parents who have formed a support group for anyone who has experienced the loss of a child through stillbirth, miscarriage, or newborn death. Our mission is to reach out to those who have experienced such a loss and provide support. www.psofpugetsound.org

Pay it Forward Dedicated to keeping our children's memory alive is through committing acts of kindness, hoping these acts will touch hearts so deeply they will also commit acts of kindness. www.payitforwardtheangelofgraceproject.org

Remembering Our Babies provides support to those who have suffered a miscarriage, ectopic pregnancy, a stillbirth, or the loss of an infant. Also is the 'collector' of events around the world for Pregnancy and Infant Loss and October 15th. www.october15th.com

Sands Promotes awareness and understanding following the death of a baby from conception through infancy. Newsletters, provides links to regional support groups, offers support, training, and resources. Australia: www.sands.org.au   New Zealand: www.sands.org.nz UK: www.uk-sands.org

SHARE Offers support groups, newsletter, chats, awareness events, and more. www.nationalshareoffice.com

SIDS and KIDS Australia, Offers bereavement support and counseling for families who have experienced stillbirth or the sudden and unexpected death of a child, whatever the cause, from 20 weeks gestation to 6 years of age. www.sidsandkids.org

Star Legacy Foundation Supports research, education, and advocacy. One of the few organizations that really does support research, brings researchers together, and even conducts some research on cause/ prevention.   Offers CEU programs online and sponsors community Reach out programs that give Parent Advocate/Loss Doula support at the time of loss and afterwards. Accepts donations and uses them well. www.starlegacyfoundation.org

Threads of Love Many chapters in the US that provide a packet showing God's love—includes a free bonnet, dress, blanket, and a prayer for healing a broken heart...for tiny infants who are sick or who have died.   Hospitals receive these and give them out for free. www.threadsoflove.org

Trisomy 18 Foundation Offers decision-making help, support, research, awareness and education. www.trisomy18.org.

Tapestry Books PO Box 6448 Hillsborough, NJ 08844, (800) 765-2367. Offers extensive catalog of hundreds of books on adoption, infertility, and infant loss. www.tapestrybooks.com

EMPTY ARMS

INFERTILITY

Hannah's Prayer An organization with Christian emphasis, concentrating on infertility or the loss of a child any time from conception through infancy. Local support chapters, newsletter and pen pal connections. www.hannah. org

RESOLVE, Inc. (888) 623-0744. Support, resources, education, and information concerning infertility. Publishes newsletter and has many local chapters. www.resolve.org

ADOPTION

National Adoption Center (800) 862-3678. Information and referral service for special needs adoption. Has state resource lists of adoption agencies, parent and advocacy groups. The Adoption Exchange matches families looking to adopt children with special needs. www.adopt.org

National Adoption Information Information Clearinghouse 1250 Maryland Avenue, SW, 8th Floor, Washington, DC 20024 (888) 251-0075 Distributes information on all areas of adoption. http://naic.acf.hhs.gov

MULTIPLES

Triplet Connection (435) 851-1105. An international network of caring and sharing for multiple birth families-expectant parents of triplets and higher-order multiple births. Newsletter, annual convention, and support, including for families who have had one or more children die in a multiple pregnancy. www.tripletconnection.org

Twin to Twin Transfusion Provides immediate and lifesaving educational, emotional and financial support to families, medical professionals, and other caregivers before, during, and after a diagnosis of twin-to-twin transfusion syndrome. Provides NICU, special needs and bereavement support. www. tttsfoundation.org

Additional Websites

www.angelnames.org - Helps with end of life expenses for babies.

www.members.shaw.ca/angelwhispers - Angel Whispers has email support, resources, newsletter, care packages, keepsakes for bereaved parents after birth, miscarriage, molar or ectopic pregnancy, or stillbirth.

http://www.babyloss.com - Online community offering information and support for bereaved parents who have suffered the death of a baby through miscarriage, ectopic pregnancy, intra-uterine death, stillbirth or other types of pregnancy loss.

www.babyphotoretouch.com - Bereavement baby photo retouching service.

www.benotafraid.net - Outreach to those who choose to continue a pregnancy.

www.aheartbreakingchoice.com - Outreach to those who choose to terminate a wanted pregnancy due to severe or lethal birth defects.

www.myforeverchild.com - Provides personalized remembrance jewelry and keepsakes honoring babies who have died.

www.geocities.com/Heartland/Bluffs/7102 -Supports Spanish speaking families.

www.glowinthewoods.com - A place where grieving parents can visit to blog.

www.griefnet.org - Internet support for dealing with grief, death and major loss. 37 email support groups and 2 web sites, including kids (http://kidsaid.com).

www.HealingFromtheStart.com - Promotes guidance for medical caregivers on how to help families when a baby dies.

www.NowILayMeDowntoSleep.org – Helps with free professional photography prior to and at the time of the loss.

www.perinatalhospice.org - Helps prepare families who know their baby will die, help create birth plans, care for baby while dying and afterwards.

www.pregnancyandinfantloss.org - Offers activities from around the world that promote education and awareness, especially during October Awareness Month and October 15th Awareness Day.

www.missingangel.org - Stillbirth board, community/ online picture memorial.

www.storknet.com - Provides information and support for pregnant parents and anyone faced with pregnancy loss or the death of a baby. Chat board and answers questions by a panel in the area of pregnancy loss.

www.spals.com - Subsequent pregnancy after loss support.

www.tearsfoundation.org - Financial support for funeral expenses – working to create chapters in every state.

BIBLIOGRAPHY

Bereaved Parent Support

After the Loss of your Baby: For Teen Mothers, Connie Nygiel, Centering Corporation, 2002. Provides information and loving support to the teenage mother. Presents risks involved in another teen pregnancy and the importance in grieving in order to heal physically and mentally, and to consider how future pregnancy should fit into your life.

Celebrating Pregnancy Again, Franchesca Cox, 2013. A journey from loss to subsequent pregnancy, with encouragement on how to handle the "new normal" that rocks your world after facing a loss.

The Anguish of Loss, Julie Fritsch with Sherokee Ilse, Wintergreen Press, 1988/1997. The ultimate resource to sensitize all who want to understand the turbulence of loss and grief. This journey, through a mother's sculptures and prose after her son's death, transcends cultures, language, history and time itself.

Anna: A Daughter's Life, Wm Loizeaux, Arcade, 1993. A beautiful, painful father's memoir of an infant daughter's life & death.

Another Baby? Maybe. Thirty Most Frequently Asked Subsequent Pregnancy Questions, Sherokee Ilse, Maribeth Doerr, Wintergreen Press, 1996. The authors, who have lived through a number of pregnancies after their own losses, share the most common concerns, issues and questions parents face when considering another pregnancy and living through it.

Bereaved Parent Survival Guide, Juliet Cassuto Rothman, Continuum Books, 1997. Comprehensive examination of the issue of parental grief, all ages of children, particularly older children. It begins with a theoretical approach.

Caring for Your Own Dead, Lisa Carlson, Upper Access Publishers, One Upper Access Rd., PO Box 457, Hinesburg, VT 05461, 1987/1997. A complete guide for those who wish to handle funeral arrangements themselves, a final act of love.

Born to Fly-An Infant's Journey to God, Cindy Claussen, A Place to Remember, 2006. Simple, beautiful, poignant...this book tells Nathan's story as he is born still then returns to God and awaits his parents coming.

Comfort Us Lord-Our Baby Died, Rev. Norman Hagley, Centering Corp. A tender book of prayers for families whose baby has died, including miscarriage.

Comforting Those Who Grieve, Doug Manning, In-Sight Books. This practical book offers caring ways to help those in mourning. Common sense and a deep faith are blended in this insightful guide.

Coming to Term: Uncovering the Truth about Miscarriage, John Cohen, Sandra Carson, MD, Houghton Mifflin, 2005. Offers detailed information about how and why miscarriages occur.

Coping with Infant or Fetal Loss: The couple's healing process, Kathleen Gilbert, Ph.D.,Laura Smart, Ph.D., Brunner Publishers, 1992. Offers specific, useful suggestions for helping couples resolve their grief and reduce stress on their relationship, along with other valuable advice.

Coping with Holidays and Celebrations, Sherokee Ilse, Wintergreen Press, 1993/2007. This booklet examines the difficulty one faces on holidays or at family gatherings after the loss of a child and offers suggestions to turn those days of difficulty toward inner reflection and even celebration of the child.

Coping with Sudden Infant Death, John De Frain, Lexington Books, 1982. A very thorough and well written book on SIDS.

Couple Communication After a Baby Dies: Differing Perspectives, Sherokee Ilse, Tim Nelson, www.wintergreenpress. com, 2008. Practical advice, wise suggestions to ponder, stories that inspire couples to talk and encourage understanding of each other's unique coping styles. A helpful and unique book that includes Tim and Monica and David and Sherokee's journey and lessons.

Dear Cheynne: A Journey into Grief..., Joanne Cacciatore, 1996/2002. www.missfoundation.org, Offers a pregnancy journal including the death of the baby, self-help skills, couples, poetry, and more.

EMPTY ARMS

Peace and Remembrance: A Guide for Parents Whose Baby Dies in the NICU, RTS. A 34 page booklet written for parents whose children die in the neonatal intensive care unit. Issues like telling other children the news, dealing with medical staff, and making funeral arrangements are all covered.

Don't Take My Grief Away From Me, Doug Manning, In-Sight Books Inc., PO Box 2058, Hereford, TX 79045. An excellent practical, supportive, and informative book for grieving family members.

Dreams of You Memory Book, Kelly Gerken, Sufficient Grace Ministries for Women, 2008. A baby memory book for babies who have died, soft graphics.

Empty Arms: Coping with Miscarriage, Stillbirth and Infant Death, Sherokee Ilse, Wintergreen Press, 1982/2008/2013/2016. A unique and encouraging book reaching out to all who have been touched by infant death. Given immediately to families in hospitals and clinics, this compassionate guide invites bereaved parents to make their own choices and decisions, but offers guidance and reasons for each decision. Available in Spanish.

Empty Cradle, Broken Heart, Deborah Davis, Fulcrum Publishing, 1996. Practical information on the early loss issues, including couples and subsequent pregnancy.

For Better or Worse, For Couples Whose Child has Died, Maribeth Wilder Doerr, Centering Corp, 1992. A short, but helpful guide to better understand common reactions by men and women, offering encouragement to communicate for better understanding.

Free to Grieve, Maureen Rank, Bethany House Publishing, 1988. Offers Christian guidance to grieving families after miscarriage and stillbirth.

From Sorrow to Serenity, Susan Fletcher, Hunter House Publications, 1998. Biblical daily affirmations to support families whose baby has died.

Grief Unseen: Healing Pregnancy Loss through the Arts, Laura Seftel, Jessica Kingsley Publishers, www.jkp.com, 2006. Through visual and literary examples, bereaved parents learn ways they can shape their sorrow into meaningful creative expressions to help them heal.

A Guide for Fathers, Tim Nelson, A Place to Remember, 2004/2007. The author shares his experience after his daughter's stillbirth, then adds his 10 year perspective on what went well, how he grieved and healed. One of very few resources that deals openly with grief from a dad's view. Bullet pointers for dads.

Healing Together: For Couples Grieving the Death of Their Baby, Marcia Tister, Sandia Torrell, Centering Corp., 1991. For couples whose baby dies, a book that covers memorial services to communication. Ends with "Letting Grief Strengthen Your Relationship."

Hope is Like the Sun: Finding Hope and Healing After Miscarriage, Stillbirth, or Infant Death, Lisa Church, HopeXchange Publishing, 2004. Like a mini support group in a book, the pages are full of wise thoughts, questions and suggestions to ponder, and places to write about your loss, especially miscarriage.

How to Prevent Miscarriage and Other Crises of Pregnancy, Stefan Semchyshyn, MD, Carol Colman, Wiley, 1990. Explores causes of miscarriage and premature labor and offers sound advice on treatment and prevention.

I'll Hold You in Heaven, Jack Hayford. Offers spiritual guidance after a baby dies and reminds them of the promise of holding them in heaven.

Infertility: The Emotional Journey, Michelle Fryer Hanson, Fairview Publishing, 1994. Stories of individuals' struggles with infertility, exploring different treatment options, family dynamics, and other emotional components.

Life Touches Life: A Mother's Story of Stillbirth and Healing, Lorraine Ash, New Sage Press, 2004. One mother's poignant story of her painful journey that leads to 'brilliant light of faith, hope and eternal love.'

Men and Grief: A Guide for Men Surviving the Death of a Loved One, Carol Staudacher, New Harbinger Publications, 1991. Explores and identifies the major characteristics of men's grief, how they cope and facilitate their grief as well as presents examples or how to take care of themselves in grief.

Men Don't Cry, Women Do, T.L. Martin, K.J.Doka, Brunner, 1999. Looks at the ways that men and women differ in expression of grief, and proposes the framework of instrumental and intuitive grieving styles.

Mending the Torn Fabric: For Those Who Grieve and Those Who Want to Help them, Sarah Brabant, Baywood Company, 1996. For professionals and the lay person, this is a compassionate account of one of the most basic issues in life, the grieving process.

Miscarriage: A Shattered Dream, Sherokee Ilse, Linda Hammer Burns, Wintergreen Press, 1985/2002/2014. A comprehensive guide on miscarriage-the medical and emotional aspects. Short, comprehensive, with a personal touch to a sensitive subject, given out in hospitals/clinics.

Miscarriage, Joy, Marv Johnson, Centering Corporation, 1988. This booklet deals with the validity of feelings, the value of the loss, family relationships, and marital issues. Available in Spanish

Miscarriage: A Man's Book, Rick Wheat, Centering Corporation, 1995. Written by a marriage and family therapist who has experienced the difficulties of miscarriage first hand, it begins with an emergency page (items a man should know right away when his wife has a miscarriage).

Miscarriage-Women Sharing from the Heart, Marie Alen, Shelly Marks, Wiley Press, 1993. Available from ICEA. Comprehensive and human, with personal stories, suggestions and research on feelings.

Mother Care: Physical Care and Beyond After a Baby Dies, S. Ilse, I. Anderson, M. Funk, Wintergreen Press, 1995/2002. A 20 page guide for new mothers on how to care for themselves after their baby dies. Focuses on the physical, emotional and spiritual healing. Give to newly bereaved moms immediately.

Mourning Sarah: A Case for Testing Group B Strep, Theresa Vigour, Radcliff, 2008. Sarah didn't need to die. If Theresa had been tested and treated for Group B Strep, Sarah probably would have lived. The story is compelling and poignant.

Ocaso Sin Aurora, Marta Steifel Ayala, Marie Ford, Centering Corp. A Spanish short guide after miscarriage & infant death.

Planning A Precious Goodbye, Sherokee Ilse, Susan Erling Martinez, Wintergreen Press, 1984/1995/2015. Short, comprehensive guide for writing an obituary, sending birth/death announcements, planning a funeral for babies, includes miscarriage. Songs, poems, prose, readings and scripture.

The Power of Positive Thinking, Norman Vincent Peale, Ballant Books, 1996. Promotes positive, hopeful thinking.

Pregnancy After a Loss, Carol Cirulli Lanham, Berkley Books, 1999. Emotional and medical advice guide parents toward and through a subsequent pregnancy.

Preventing Miscarriage-The Good News, Jonathon Scher MD, Carol Dix, Harper/Row, 1990. Explains why some pregnancies fail, medical tests to pinpoint potential causes, and latest treatments available to prevent some losses in pregnancies. Not a cure all, but good information.

Remembering with Love: Messages of Hope for the First Year of Grieving and Beyond, Sherokee Ilse, Elizabeth Levang, Ph.D, Fairview Press, 1992. An uplifting, daily affirmation book based on real scenarios of people who have had a loved one die. A readers guide at the beginning offers assistance in locating the topic or issue being faced at the moment.

Remembering Our Angels, Hannah Stone, Lulu.com, 2007. A compilation of pieces written by doctors, therapists, and bereaved parents, this book shares wisdom and many citations for further exploration.

Saul. Kay, R St. Martin's, 2000. A story of a mom's son was born extremely prematurely and died four months later. Offers a unique perspective that a baby's experience was part of his or her unique and ultimately spiritual path.

SIDS Survival Guide, Joani Heckler, Robin Moris, 1994. The information is interlaced with heartrending personal experiences and poetry supplied by family members who responded to Horchler's call for contributions through parent support groups. Many resources are cited.

A Silent Sorrow: Pregnancy Loss, Guidance and Support for You and Your Family, Ingrid Kohn, MSW, Perry-Lynn Moffitt, Dell, 1993. Covers most aspects of pregnancy loss in a compassionate manner (over 400 pages). Excellent for families and care providers.

Single Parent Grief, Sherokee Ilse, A Place to Remember, 1994/2009. For teens or a more mature parent, this resource explores the special grief of single parents who have no steady partner. Suggestions and information offer hope, a good resource section included.

Still to be Born, Pat Schwiebert, Perinatal Loss/Grief Watch, 1986/2000. Parents' stories of subsequent pregnancies after loss, medical considerations, emotional issues, and more are presented in this book.

Strong and Tender, Pat Schwiebert, Perinatal Loss/Grief Watch, 1996/2003. This practical booklet helps dads understand the grief work they need to do and how to find their own way of expressing their sorrow.

Surviving Miscarriage: You are Not Alone, Stacy MacLaughlin, iUniverse, inc, 2005. Shares miscarriage experiences. A thirty-day plan guides readers through meaningful steps to help banish shame, embrace comforting. emotional recovery, and move forward with hope.

Surviving Pregnancy Loss, Rochelle Friedman, MD, Bonnie Gradstein, MD, Little Brown & Co., 1982. The book provides a comprehensive discussion of the physical and emotional consequences of pregnancy loss.

Tear Soup, Pat Schweibert, Grief Watch, 2005. For all ages including children. this story and beautiful pictures offers a sweet 'recipe for healing after loss.'

Tender Miscarriage: An Epiphany, Paula Saffire, Harbinger House, 1989. A gentle story of love and loss written to the little baby who died and the millions who share such a tragic journey.

They Were Still Born, edited by Janel Atlas. Moving short pieces from many authors and parent advocates whose children were 'still born'. Also has a significant section on stillbirth causes and prevention including emerging research - on cord/placenta problems, fetal growth restriction, infection, decreased movement/kick counting, and more.

Trying Again: A Guide to Pregnancy after Miscarriage, Stillbirth, and Infant Death, Ann Douglas, Taylor Publishing, 2000. Provides considerations to help decide whether one is emotionally and physically ready to try for another pregnancy...what to expect when trying again and problems one may encounter.

How to Make it Meaningful, Ashley Davis Prend, Berkely Books, 1997. One of the few books that gives support for the importance of grief's ongoing impact and how it changes through the years.

Understanding Mourning, Glen Davidson, Augsburg Publishing, 1984. Easy to understand, based on sound research, this book gives you definite ideas on how to mourn well and how to understand others who are mourning.

Unsupported Losses: Blighted Ovum, Ectopic and Molar Pregnancies, Sherokee Ilse, A Place to Remember, 1994. This booklet addresses the complicating factors surrounding these often ignored losses, offering emotional support and an understanding of medical implications.

We Lost Our Baby: One couple's Story of Miscarriage and its Aftermath, Siobhan O'Neill-White, David White, Liffey Press, 2008, www.theliffeypress.com. A personal look into the heart of a couple who had a miscarriage.

When A Baby Dies, Rana Limbo, Sarah Wheeler, RTS, 1989. Stories of families and clinical information for caregivers, includes checklists.

When Hello Means Goodbye, Pat Schwiebert, Paul Kirk, Perinatal Loss, 1977/2007, www.griefwatch.com. One of the first booklets written for bereaved families; practical and full of advice from people who have been there.

When Pregnancy Follows a Loss, Joann O'Leary, Claire Thorwick 2006, available through wintergreenpress.com. Addresses the conflicting emotions of living through another pregnancy and shares many families' stories.

A Woman Doctor's Guide to Miscarriage: Essential Facts and Up-to-the Minute Inforrnation on Coping with Pregnancy Loss and Trying Again, Irene Daria, Laurie Abkemeier, Lynn Friedman, vol. I, 1996.

Pregnancy Complications

Bedrest Before Baby: What's a Mother to Do? A Survival Handbook for High-Risk Moms, Patricia Isennock, Mustardseed, (800) 299-3366, 1992. Describes some of the feelings shared by women on pregnancy bedrest, offering practical help on such strategies as how to pay medical bills and how to relieve the boredom of bedrest.

Every Pregnant Woman's Guide to Preventing Preterm Birth, Barbara Like, Times Books, 1995. Practical, scientifically sound information on risk factors identified with prematurity and how to reduce them.

For the Love of Angela, Nancy Mayer-Whittington, St. Catherine of Siena Press, www.fortheloveofangela.com 2007. Nancy shares her story of continuing her pregnancy with her daughter who had Trisomy 18 which usually results in death before or shortly after birth.

How to Prevent Miscarriages and Other Crises of Pregnancy, Stefan Semchyshyn, MD, Carol Coleman, Collier, 1990. Addresses some causes of miscarriage and premature labor, then offers sound, state of the art advice on potential treatment options.

Loving and Letting Go: For Parents Who Decided to Turn Away from Aggressive Medical Intervention for Their Critically Ill Newborn, Deborah Davis, Centering Corp, 1993. For parents who decide to reject aggressive medical intervention for their critically ill newborns.

A Mother's Dilemma: A Spiritual Search for Meaning Following Pregnancy Interruption After Prenatal Diagnosis, Wendy Lyon, Molly Minnick, www.pineapplebooks.com.. About forgiveness of self, each other, and God after ending a wanted pregnancy.

Precious Lives, Painful Choices: A Prenatal Decision-Making Guide, Sherokee Ilse, Wintergreen Press, 1993/eBook 2016. A comprehensive, balanced guide to assist families in their struggle with abnormal prenatal results. To be given immediately upon diagnosis to aid in decision-making.

A Time to Decide, A Time to Heal, Molly Minnick, Kathleen Delp, Pineapple Press. Booklet mostly to support parents who terminate their pregnancy after poor prenatal diagnosis, covers continuing, and subsequent pregnancy.

Waiting with Gabriel, Amy Kubelbeck, Loyola Press, 2003. A gentle story of a family who chose to continue their pregnancy for 3 ½ months as they waited to meet their son who would die.

When Pregnancy Isn't Perfect, Laurie Rich, Dutton Books, 1996. A layperson's guide to complications in pregnancy, written by a mother who went through a high-risk pregnancy. A classic that deals with medical and emotional issues.

Helping Children Cope

Am I Still a Big Sister? Audrey B. Weir, Fallen Press, 1992. Amanda's baby sister Rachel dies in the hospital. Offers information and comfort.

Helping Children Cope with the Loss of a Loved One, Dr. William Koren, Free Spirit Press, 1996. With clear and concise language, the author offers comfort, compassion and sound advice. He explains how children from infancy through age 18 perceive and react to death and offers suggestions to help children live through loss.

How Do We Tell the Children: A Parent's Guide to Helping Children Understand and Cope When Someone Dies, Don Schaefer and Christine Lyons, New Market Press, 1994. Provides straight forward, uncomplicated language to help parents explain death to children from two years to the teenage years.

Lifetimes: A Beautiful Way to Explain Death to Children, Bryan Mellonie, Robert Ingpen, Bantam Books, 1983. Explains how all living things have beginnings and endings.

Molly's Rosebush, Janice Cohn, Albert Whitman & Co., 1995. One of the nicest children's books available on miscarriage. Fully illustrated in pastels, this real life story openly confronts the fears that might affect siblings after a miscarriage.

EMPTY ARMS

No New Baby, Marilyn Bryte, Centering Corp., 1988. For siblings when a baby brother or sister dies through miscarriage.

Sibling Grief, Sherokee Ilse, Linda Hammer Burns, Wintergreen Press, 1985/1996/2009. A practical guide to help parents understand their surviving children'sneeds and to assist them in grieving and coping with their brother or sister's death.

Someone Came Before You, Pat Schweibert, Grief Watch. A book for children who come after the death of a sibling.

Stacy Had a Little Sister, Wendie Old. A Place to Remember. Stacy has mixed feelings about a new sister, then the baby dies of SIDS.

Thumpy's Story: A Story of Love and Grief Shared, Nancy Dodge, SHARE, 1985. A story book, workbook, and video that tells a story of a sibling bunny's death in a very gentle and understanding way.

We Were Going to have a Baby, but We had an Angel Instead, Pat Schweibert, Grief Watch. Helps children whose parents have a pregnancy loss.

Where's Jess? Centering Corp. An excellent book for siblings after their neonatal baby brother or sister dies.

OTHER BOOKS BY WINTERGREEN PRESS

The Anguish of Loss portrays normal human emotions after loss. It transcends time, history, cultures, educational levels, and all nationalities. A true classic! A photographic journey of a mother's anguish portrayed in a series of powerful sculptures. A gift to all experiencing grief and to others seeking that depth of emotional understanding! $14.95

The Anguish of Loss slide show/DVD is available for rent ($45) or purchase ($100)

Another Baby? Maybe... The authors, who have lived through a number of pregnancies after their own losses, share the most common concerns and questions parents face as they consider and/or live through another pregnancy. $5.00

Couple Communication After a Baby Dies, Sherokee and Tim Nelson. Never before has such a book been written that is so personal and real. Grounded in sensible philosophies, the authors, with over the 20+ years of their marriages (to David and Monica), share their stories and offer suggestions after each couple's baby died. $12.95

Miscarriage: A Shattered Dream offers support and guidance for those who have suffered a miscarriage as well as for their professional caregivers, family members, and friends. This comprehensive guide is thorough and well written. ISBN 0-960945-3-6 $12.95

Planning a Precious Goodbye, Sherokee and Susan Erling. This short, yet comprehensive guide for writing an obituary, sending announcements, planning a memorial or funeral service offers prose, poetry, songs, and scripture, and readings. $4.50 (This booklet can also be downloaded immediately onto your computer at www.MemorEmedia.com).

For more information, more books and booklets, or to order contact:

Wintergreen Press   www.wintergreenpress.com

email: sherokeeilse@yahoo.com

14108 North Biltmore Drive, Oro Valley, AZ 85755

(952) 476-1303

A NOTE FROM THE AUTHOR

I welcome your comments about this book—suggestions for improving it and/or your personal experiences. Please know that I read each letter that is sent to me and make every effort to write back, though there will be times in my life where this may not be possible. My heart goes out to you in your pain or as you help someone who is in pain.

If you have suggestions of groups, hospitals, professional care providers, libraries, or bookstores who might want copies of this book, or any of my titles, please let me know and feel free to make the suggestion to them.

Thank you,

Sherokee

Please write to me at:
Sherokee Ilse

sherokeeilse@yahoo.com   www.wintergreenpress.com